Living with Your Husband's
Secret Wars

MARSHA MEANS

Fleming H. Revell
A Division of Baker Book House Co
Grand Rapids, Michigan 49516

Published by Fleming H. Revell
a division of Baker Book House Company
P.O. Box 6287, Grand Rapids, MI 49516-6287

Fifth printing, February 2003

Printed in the United States of America

Library of Congress Cataloging-in-Publication Data

Means, Marsha, 1948–
    Living with your husband's secret wars / Marsha Means.
       p.   cm.
    Includes bibliographical references.
    ISBN 0-8007-5710-6 (pbk.)
    1. Wives—Religious life. 2. Husbands—Sexual behavior. 3. Sex addiction—Religious aspects—Christianity. 4. Adultery. I. Title.
BV4527.M435   1999
248.4'8435 21—dc21   99-041564

For current information about all releases from Baker Book House, visit our web site:
http://www.bakerbooks.com

Living with Your Husband's
Secret Wars

For Troy and Tricia—
I wish I could do it all again, but with no mistakes.

And for my life partner and dearest friend, Pat.
You are God's gift to me, the love of my life,
and all I ever dreamed a husband could be.

Contents

Acknowledgments

The books I value most are the ones that help me understand and deal with my own human experience as I see my hopes and fears, my faith and doubt, my joy and pain reflected in the life stories of other people. It is my prayer that this will be that kind of book for you and that you will find yourself somewhere in these pages.

This book is a compilation of the stories of dozens of women whose husbands have struggled with some kind of "secret war." A few have given permission to use their real names. In most cases, these women and their husbands now have public ministries to other couples going through the pain of an extramarital affair or the discovery of a husband's sexual struggles or addiction. Information on how to contact these dedicated couples may be found in appendix 3. Among these, I want to express my gratitude to Elizabeth Harris, Marnie Ferree, Sharon Hersh, Earl and Sandy Wilson, Carol Anderson and Jim Shores, and Pamela and Richard Crist.

I am grateful, too, to Juanita Ryan for granting me permission to include several of her exquisitely crafted poems. Juanita has a gift for capturing both the joy and the pain that sometimes accompany intimate relationships. Juanita, who is a counselor, is also listed in appendix 3.

My special thanks goes to Jon and Anita T., our dear friends, for allowing us to tell their story. Anita was also an invaluable touchstone for me at several points in the development of the manuscript. Thank you, Anita.

Acknowledgments

I'm also grateful to the dozens of women who have shared their stories with us anonymously. I've carefully altered details and names to protect these women's identities.

Above all, I'm deeply grateful to Pat, my husband and partner in ministry and life, for his encouragement and help along the way.

It is my hope that by reading these stories, you will find the strength and courage you need to walk the particular journey toward healing that God has placed before you.

Introduction

Crazy Time

"*My husband and* I are the youth leaders at our church, and he's had three affairs. I don't know how much longer I can go on."

"My husband is a Christian, and he's having an affair with a woman he met on the Internet. I don't know how to get him to stop."

"My husband is a pastor, and I found three hard-core pornographic videos behind the headboard in our bedroom. Since then our lives have been turned upside down."

Unfortunately, this is not fiction. In the last two years I've heard more of these stories from Christian women than I ever thought possible. It was two years ago that my husband, Pat, wrote *Men's Secret Wars*. His book tells how he lost the battle with sexual sin in his first marriage. It also tells how, a decade later, God has given him a speaking and writing ministry to warn men about the secret sins that can destroy their lives. Scores of Christian radio stations across the country have interviewed him since writing the book, and following every interview, our phone begins ringing. Most of the callers are women who have recently discovered her husband's secret war. Each has her own painful story, but all the stories share one thing in common: After discovering her husband's sexual sin, the woman is swept into a tornado of emotion. She feels wrenched from her familiar world and spun into a grief cycle, very much as if someone she loves has just died. One woman described those feelings this way:

> I felt thrust into emotional shock. I experienced disbelief, hurt, loss—it felt like this couldn't be happening. My life went into slow motion, like in a movie when the voices and pictures seem to be drenched in molasses. It was a crazy time that left my emotions fluctuating wildly from day to day, and even hour to hour. This period lasted for several days, maybe a couple of weeks. My husband couldn't understand why I didn't just bounce back. "I don't understand why you haven't moved on," he said to me. But it isn't that easy. Something precious and sacred that belonged to me was given to someone else, and I felt overwhelmed by grief and loss.
>
> During this time I really needed to talk about my feelings, but I didn't know who would understand and keep it confidential. I had a praise tape with the song "Lay Your Burdens at the Foot of the Cross" on it; for days I lay on the sofa in the living room and played the tape over and over again. I pictured myself laying my pain at the foot of the cross. I did begin to feel Christ's comfort as I listened. If I could meet those musicians, I would tell them how they ministered to me there in my living room.

The initial period after discovering a husband's sexual sin often feels like a "crazy time" to the women I talk to. While reactions vary—some experience rage immediately, others don't until later—that world-is-turned-upside-down feeling is the same for each woman. They are experiencing the beginning of the grief process. It's not a one-two-three process, but a tumultuous time filled with emotional peaks and valleys.

If you or someone you care about is dealing with the pain that mental or physical infidelity brings, know that as much as it hurts, feeling the pain is an important part of the healing. During this time, a woman needs the chance to focus on taking care of herself and to talk about what she's feeling. She needs to take time to grieve—to journal, cling to the Bible's promises, listen to praise music, do the things she finds most comforting, and be reminded that it won't *always* hurt this much.

As I've talked to many, many women, felt their hurt and pain, and heard their cries for help, I've learned more about the dark, painful world of sexual addiction. Since hearing the stories of numerous couples, I now know this world encompasses a wide spectrum of secret behaviors: habitual lust and fantasizing, addiction to pornography, maintaining secret friendships on the Internet, frequenting prostitutes, engaging in affairs, incest, or child molestation, to name a few. Until now, I had no idea how many Christian men become entangled in some form of seemingly uncontrollable sexual activity. *Living with Your Husband's Secret Wars* tells the stories of many of these men's wives and other women I've worked with as well. While I've never personally experienced the agony created when a husband has an affair, I do struggle with trust issues because Pat had an affair during his first marriage. I have also felt all the fears that come with the knowledge that there is absolutely nothing I can do to keep my husband from being tempted in our sexually saturated society.

In one of those serendipities that sometimes occur in life, I have found new strength for my own marriage as I have listened to the painful stories told by so many other women. This process has forced me to confront my total helplessness in controlling my husband and to instead surrender my marriage each day to God. I then focus on my own emotional and spiritual growth and the broken places in my character.

After months of research, a route I could follow to foster this personal growth began to emerge. This book presents that route, but it's not always a straight road. It usually includes many twists and turns and doubling back as we toil along its path. You may not follow it in the exact sequence it's presented here, but the destination remains the same. We are traveling together to a place of hope, healing, and new beginnings. Whether you make the journey alone or with the man in your life, it is my prayer that you find help within these pages for your own pilgrimage.

— 1 —

Discovering Your Husband's Secret War

Surviving the Unthinkable

> Sometimes the emptiness will be so deep, you will almost be able to feel the wind blowing through the place where your heart should be.
>
> *Robin Norwood,*
> *Women Who Love Too Much*

The last shimmering gold of a Riviera sunset melted on the Mediterranean as Julie studied her husband's face across the resort's restaurant table. Even the hint of premature graying at his temples didn't detract from his youthful good looks. She could still see the nineteen-year-old she fell in love with behind the strong masculine lines and mahogany brown eyes.

They fell in love as undergraduates. He felt God calling him to pastor, and she planned to teach. Over the next four years they shared every moment they could. Dating, attending church, and long hours studying in the library filled the months that quickly passed. As they fell more deeply in love, they knew someday they would marry. But Dick felt they should wait until he finished seminary and they were financially stable, so Julie waited as patiently as her heart would let her.

And then finally the long wait was over. They prepared their first home, had a beautiful family wedding, and flew to France for a dream-come-true honeymoon—a wedding gift from their parents. They felt certain theirs must be the deepest, strongest love God ever created.

Julie looked across the restaurant table and searched Dick's eyes for the loving response she'd come to anticipate. Instead, she saw his sultry gaze fixed somewhere behind her left shoulder. His eyes darted nervously back to hers when he caught her watchful look. She felt the sting of pain and anger as she realized that his look was intended for someone else. Glancing down at her plate, she forced herself to keep talking and ignore his action.

Hoping for reassurance, she looked up at him once again. His eyes reflected that look of desire all women know. But it wasn't intended for her. Her heart felt heavy and dead in her chest.

Again his eyes nervously met hers with mock attentiveness. Then a third and fourth time they played out their little drama. Finally, she could stand it no longer. She turned to see who held his attention and recognized a young, strikingly beautiful, raven-haired hotel guest. She felt a cold knife slice through her soul.

Many times during their long courtship she pretended not to notice when he stared at attractive women, even though it hurt her. She felt certain that when they were married, he'd be completely satisfied with her and this habit would stop. But this time she couldn't ignore it. It was too obvious and hurtful. Making some excuse, Julie left the table and hurried to their room, fighting hard not to cry in front of the other guests.

Alone in their room, she leaned against the wall and held herself, sobbing. Pulling off her clothes, she stepped into the shower and turned on the hot water. But the pain wouldn't wash away. She felt humiliated, angry, hurt, and insulted—all at the same time.

Several minutes later, Dick came back to the room.

"What's wrong, Julie? I couldn't figure out why you didn't come back."

Trembling, she took a deep breath and tried to remain calm. "I need for you to be honest and open with me about what was going on in the restaurant. I'm tired of you giving that sexy look to attractive women."

"Don't be ridiculous. You know I'm just a people watcher," he lied.

"Dick, that wasn't harmless people watching. We both know that." She could hear her voice shaking and getting louder but couldn't seem to control it. "Don't lie to me! We're on our *honeymoon*—how could you do that?"

"Are you finished?" he asked angrily, then turned, opened the door, and walked out of their room. Julie felt alone and confused, abandoned and betrayed, and didn't know what else to do but pray and try to sleep.

She was more fortunate than many women. After a night of thought and prayer, Dick humbly apologized. "I'm sorry for the pain I caused you, honey. I know I was wrong, and I'm really sorry I hurt you. Lust is a pattern I can't seem to break, and I need to do something about it. I'm going to begin working with a counselor when we get home," he said.

Instead of responding graciously to his apology, Julie exploded with more hurt and anger. She threw an ashtray at him, called him names, and stormed out of the room. The next day they decided to change their flight and go home early, ending their wonderful honeymoon trip. During the long hours on the plane, they barely spoke; each suffered alone in silence.

I'm discovering that Julie's story isn't unique. From the calls we receive and from surveys and studies done by others, I know there are thousands of Christian couples in the church who live in similar situations. Fuller Institute of Church Growth's 1991 survey of pastors showed that 37 percent of the respondents had been involved in inappropriate sexual behavior with someone in their church.[1] And *Christianity Today*'s 1992 survey of one thousand subscribers indicated that 49 percent had viewed pornography in the past year (only a small portion of the respondents were women).[2]

Before we're married, no one tells women what a common problem this is, even among Christian men. But just what is taking place in these habitual sexual behaviors? Many professionals call it sexual addiction.

What Is Sexual Addiction?

"Sexual addiction is a sickness involving any type of uncontrollable sexual activity,"[3] says author and Christian counselor Dr. Mark Laaser. Ranging from habitual lust, using pornography, and going to topless bars, to voyeurism, exhibitionism, compulsive masturbation, repeated affairs, incest, or child molestation, a multitude of Christian men struggle with some level of this temptation—and lose the battle. One man tells how, under the guise of "people watching," he goes through a ritual of mentally undressing women. While some would argue that lust like this is not *addiction,* for women like Julie, the scientific definition of sexual addiction doesn't matter. The knowledge that her husband is involved in any type of habitual sexual behavior outside of their relationship devastates most Christian women. Many marriages have been damaged and lives destroyed by one or a combination of these behaviors.

Dr. Patrick Carnes, sexual addiction expert and author of *Out of the Shadows,* explains the man's experience.

A way to understand sexual addicts is to compare them with other types of addicts. A common definition of alcoholism or drug dependency is that a person has a pathological relationship with a mood-altering chemical. The alcoholic's relationship with alcohol becomes more important than family, friends, and work. The relationship progresses to the point where alcohol is necessary to feel normal. To feel "normal" for the alcoholic is also to feel isolated and lonely since the primary relationship he depends upon to feel adequate is a chemical, not other people. The sexual addiction is parallel. The addict substitutes a sick relationship to an event or process for a healthy relationship with others. The addict's relationship with a mood-altering "experience" becomes central to his life.[4]

The grip is as strong for men who fight lust and pornography addictions as it is for the man who fights an alcohol or drug addiction. Eric is an example of how deeply pornography's hook can sink into a man. When Eric was about twenty-two and attending Bible college in preparation for the mission field, he spent the summer in the rainy redwood forests of northern California.

> There I discovered pornography while living in a small trailer with a friend. With all the rain, there wasn't a lot to do after work, so I rationalized what I was doing, telling myself that I was an unmarried Christian man. I didn't plan to keep it up. Serving as a youth pastor back at school that fall, I told myself I needed to quit; I didn't feel right using it while ministering. But it wasn't that easy, so I played games in my head. If I was asked to speak at a church, I'd discipline myself to not view any pornography in the three or four days preceding the service. But I had already become caught up in the thrill of drinking in the pictures and lusting after even bigger fixes. I told myself it was temporary and that when I was mar-

ried I wouldn't need it anymore. I also convinced myself that the pornographic material was helping me become sexually educated.

Then I did get married and I was sure marriage would fulfill all my fantasies: Legitimate sex and nudity would always be available, and my empty void inside would be filled. I quickly found out that marriage didn't make my emptiness go away. We were just two needy kids who wanted to be rescued. That began years of cycles of highs when I anticipated the purchase of a new pornographic magazine, and lows of guilt and shame and vowing never to do it again. I'd get on my knees before God and rededicate my life and beg the Lord to help me keep my vows. But I'd always do it again.

Dr. Patrick Carnes again explains what the addict goes through: "Addicts progressively go through stages in which they retreat further from the reality of friends, family, and work. Their secret lives become more real than their public lives. What people know is a false identity. Only the individual addict knows the shame of living a double life— the real world and the addict's world."[5]

Why Does He Do It?

What is it that draws men, even Christian men, to pornography, affairs, and other types of inappropriate sexual behavior? On one level, of course, the answer is that we each possess a sin nature that pulls us toward wrong behavior. But that doesn't answer why men are drawn toward *this* type of behavior.

Eric, whose experience with pornography I just described, believes factors in his childhood were the underlying issue that propelled him toward these activities.

> I grew up in a religious, legalistic home. My parents were missionaries, but the love of Christ was not lived out in my family. Mom and Dad had a difficult marriage and they often abused us physically. My dad actually abused me sexually, as well. As far back as I can remember, I've felt sexualized—always interested in and thinking about sex and acting out sexually.

Many people who are sexually abused in early childhood are drawn into inappropriate sexual activities, sometimes when they're still very, very young. For some people, habitual sexual behavior serves as a response to stress and other factors in their adult lives. Still other men feel drawn to women for different reasons. They've been raised to have a dependency on women's approval. In his book, *Men's Secret Wars,* my husband, Pat, tells the story of Ron's temptation:

"Women run my emotions," he said angrily. "It's been that way all my life."

Ron's father had been a life-long alcoholic. A brooding, verbally abusive man, he went unemployed for long periods while Ron was growing up. Ron learned to avoid him whenever possible and sought refuge in his relationship with his mother.

"Mom and I were especially close," Ron recalled. "She'd protect me from Dad when he was drunk, and she'd tell me her secrets—things she didn't tell Dad."

Ron's mother often talked to him about her unhappiness in the marriage and about the pain she carried. Ron soon learned to comfort and reassure her. He shook his head in embarrassment when he described dozens of scenes where a dry-eyed twelve-year-old boy held his mother while she cried.

"I became her emotional caretaker," Ron said. "I could walk into the room and instantly know what mood she was in. If she was happy, I was happy. If she was down, I knew it was my job to make her happy again. It's like I didn't have an emotional life of my own.

21

"It's scary," Ron went on, "but I see the same thing happening in my adult relationships. I'd rather talk to a woman
than a man, and I always seem to end up being a friend and
counselor to some emotionally needy woman."[6]

Ron later had an affair with a woman he had comforted.

Many other men would agree with Eric and Ron about
the childhood roots of sexual addiction. But regardless what
type of sexual addiction he fights, or how it originally got
started in a man's life, it is also a spiritual problem. Sexaholics Anonymous literature explains:

> The spiritual process of addiction is the pattern of attitudes,
> beliefs, actions, and reactions that leads to an unhealthy
> dependency on something, such as a drug or a behavior. It is
> a process because it develops over time and involves the incor-
> poration of many experiences, ideas, and people. It is a spir-
> itual process because it involves your total being, your phys-
> ical, emotional, and psychic strengths, and your vital
> energies—everything that comes to you and from within you.
> Every other relationship is subjugated to your relationship to
> the addiction. Addiction is not simply physical—although
> obviously that is affected. It affects the way you think, which
> affects the way you feel, unlike needs that you depend on for
> life. Addictions are self-destructive. That is, the more you
> indulge in your addictions the more disruptive to your life
> they become.[7]

They certainly disrupt a marriage and rip at a woman's heart.

How Is the Wife Affected?

In *An Affair of the Mind*, Christian writer Laurie Hall
tells her own heartbreaking story of her husband's sexual
addiction, which began with soft-core pornography and
progressed to daily sex outside his marriage. But even when
pornography doesn't lead to a sexual relationship with

another person, it still damages a marriage. Men say that they can't help but compare their wives to the pornographic pictures they see, and for the woman that knowledge is agonizing.

Valerie, a bubbly, dimpled brunette describes the pain she felt when her husband used pornography.

> Daniel and I had gotten a babysitter and gone on a "date." We took our picnic dinner to our very favorite place—a lake near our home where we love to watch the sunset. On our drive there, Daniel started saying some things that sounded like he was talking about pornography. I could hardly believe my ears. Unbelieving, I asked him, "Are you talking about pornography? Are you telling me you've looked at pornography?" When he said yes, I just came apart. We never got out of the car. I was hurt and angry and shaking all over. "It might as well have been an affair!" I screamed at him. "I hate you! You've broken your marriage vows to me! You may not have been with a real woman, but you've already done it in your head! It tells me you don't think I'm enough!" I felt totally betrayed.

Valerie told me how she'd moved out temporarily. Ultimately she and Daniel sought help and over the next couple of bumpy years began some tough growth work that saved their marriage.

Denise, wife of Eric, whose story I told earlier, poignantly describes her reaction to her husband's addiction.

> I still remember the first time I saw *Penthouse* in Eric's truck. My pulse was pounding, and I felt white with rage. I felt like I wanted to get rid of the bum, but I couldn't live with him and I couldn't live without him. I wanted him to stay, but I also wanted him to stop

what he was doing. He did burn the magazine for me after I confronted him, but that wasn't the end of it. I felt like I was competing with women I could never be like. I felt betrayed, terribly angry—and I also felt that if he wanted those women, he'd never, ever touch me again. I tried to punish him in bed for the next few nights. I wouldn't even let our toes touch. But at the same time, it's kind of crazy how it works. I thought I had everything inside me to make him stop. I tried many different ways to be more perfect, to be more sexy, to be more beautiful, to try to prove to him that I was everything he'd ever need. But nothing worked. And I was so angry that I couldn't control his addiction. I didn't have the power to make him stop. I felt so helpless.

A woman nearly always responds to her husband's lust, pornography use, or affairs with hurt, anger, feelings of betrayal, and the belief that she isn't "woman enough" to hold her man. But we react in other ways, too.

What Are Women's Typical Responses?

Doormat Response

Some of us become doormats, accepting our husbands' behavior because we don't know what else to do. One woman told me her husband has moved out and is seeing another woman, yet she lets him come home to dinner when he wants to. Another's husband is having an affair and says mean, hurtful things about the way his wife looks, but she still gives him sex when he wants it.

"Ignore It" Response

Because it hurts so deeply, many of us try to ignore the signs and use other "coping" methods first. We may use any of several mind-blocking techniques to deny it happens, even when reality indicates it is happening.

"Normalize It" Response

Some women normalize it—saying all men do these things, so it's okay—and disregard their own feelings. That's the way my friend Wendy deals with her Christian husband's visits to topless bars. "That's the way all the men I've ever known have acted," Wendy said. "I figure that just comes with the package when you marry a man."

"Spiritualize It" Response

Many women spiritualize the problem by asking God to change their spouse, while setting about to help God do the changing. This is the most common reaction I hear from Christian women. Lynn, whose husband has been having affairs for sixteen years, told me she has horrible nightmares about eventually being left alone because her husband will leave with one of the other women. But she tells me she "had a vision, and she believes God has given her an anointing to love her husband through this."

"Get Back" Response

Others of us react in a different way. We try to "get back" by acting out sexually in an effort to hurt our husbands, to make them jealous, or to put ourselves on an even footing with them so we can stay connected because now "I'm bad, too." Colleen used this technique to deal with her hurt and anger.

> John had returned home from a business trip late one night, and because we were tired, we headed straight for bed. After he left the next morning, I decided to quickly unpack his suitcase before I left for work so

his dirty clothes wouldn't miss the laundry. As I lifted the last pair of slacks out of the suitcase, I uncovered a pornographic magazine sporting the image of a voluptuous, nearly nude blonde. I was horrified and furious. I couldn't believe my wonderful Christian husband—the man I trusted and considered my best friend in the whole world—could buy and read such garbage! I actually felt ill. Sitting down on the edge of the bed, I flipped through the magazine. Gorgeous women wearing nothing but a seductive smile and satin skin looked back at me from the glossy pages.

I didn't make it to work that day; I called in sick. And then I called John and asked if we could meet downtown for lunch. I knew I wouldn't feel like eating, but I also knew I couldn't wait until he got home to confront him.

What followed was messy and hurtful for both of us. I yelled at John and called him names. My strongest emotion was rage—I just wanted to hurt him—to get back at him somehow for his mental infidelity.

Leaving John sitting with his mouth open in shock, I drove to a fancy hotel in our city and headed for the lounge. If he could do it, so could I. He could just find out how it felt to be betrayed by the person you trust the most. So when an attractive man offered to buy me a drink, I said, "Okay, thanks," and smiled at him, ignoring my screaming conscience. Sipping my club soda, we talked for about an hour, and then he asked if I'd like to go up to his room and order room service for dinner. My heart was pounding, and I knew it was wrong, but I went. The afternoon ended when I was nearly raped.

Obviously, this reaction pattern is sin and can also be dangerous. It doesn't prove a thing, and actually makes things much worse, as it clouds the original issue that needs to be dealt with. But for some of us, it's almost an automatic response to the hurt. Similar reactions include dressing seductively, flirting with other men, choosing to become emotionally involved with another man, or going so far as to have an affair of our own. None of these actions gets us anywhere but down.

Emotional Shutdown Response

Feeling so flooded with pain that we "shut down" emotionally is another frequent reaction. Donna's husband had an affair and she feels overwhelmed emotionally.

> I can get through the mornings okay because I'm busy with getting breakfast ready, lunches packed, and seeing that everyone gets out the door on time. But when they're all gone and the house is quiet I fall apart. All I can do is sit in the middle of the living room floor and cry. It hurts so bad I can hardly stand it, but I can't seem to help myself. I don't seem to have the emotional energy to move ahead. I don't know what to do.

Others of us make it through the daytime okay, but our feelings and emotions spiral downward as bedtime approaches and the possibility of sexual activity with our spouse presents itself. Sylvia found it affected her emotional and sexual freedom after she learned about her husband's pornography addiction.

> I couldn't undress in front of him—I felt so vulnerable and exposed, even with my clothes on. I sure didn't want him to see me without clothes, and I certainly didn't want to give him a chance to compare me to the pictures he looked at. The idea of sex with him made me feel numb and dead. I just wanted to

> wear a long nightgown, get into bed, pull the covers
> over my head, and pray I'd fall asleep quickly.

Others of us may go through the motions of intimacy, but purposely disconnect from our feelings during sex. Like children who are molested, we hurt too much to stay emotionally present.

For some, the emotional shutdown response can lead to something even more dangerous.

Deep Depression and Suicidal Response

Often women feel deep, overwhelming depression, and for a few, those feelings escalate to suicidal thoughts. Veronica just wanted to end the pain when her husband had an affair with a younger woman in their church.

> I was so weary of the warfare. So tired of won-
> dering what my husband would do. It was as if I heard
> a sweet voice saying, "Three to five minutes, three to
> five minutes, and it can all be over." That night I told
> my husband to go on to bed, that I was going to stay
> up for a while. I got a sharp knife and laid down in the
> bathtub, ready to take my life. Suddenly, I felt the over-
> whelming presence of the Lord. I could almost hear
> him whisper in my heart, "I am the source of your
> hope, even in your hopeless moments." And I couldn't
> do it. I had to choose life. But it's still incredibly hard.
> You know you can go forty days without food and
> three days without water, but you can't go five min-
> utes without hope.

Nonconfrontational Response

Still others of us feel a need to escape the pain by running away. We pack suitcases and threaten divorce but never follow through. We never make a healthy separation to get help, sort through our feelings, pray, and plan a healthy confrontation. Why do we just stay, circulating through reactions, never forcing a biblical confrontation to create accountability for our husband? Waiting for him to change is far less frightening for most women than confronting him.

Many women fear the loss of their marriage. They stay because they have children and don't want them to grow up without a father, or they feel unable to support their children without their husband's help. Others say they don't think that Christians should get divorced or separated—even when adultery has been committed. Some stay, even when children are no longer at home, because they fear financial insecurity. And a few just say, "But I love him." Several women tell me they've hung on for years without confronting. In the case of one pastor's wife, it's involved seventeen years and numerous affairs.

Most of us love our husbands and fear losing them to their addiction. We often mistakenly think that if we stay, we can somehow control their activities and by doing so, keep them out of tempting situations. But this, too, can lead to problems.

"Control It" Response

Mary Anne, a woman whose husband had an affair with a much younger woman, attempts to control her husband by being his "moral monitor."

> I ask Bill to tell me where all he plans to go when he leaves the house. Because he's a salesman who goes to clients' homes, I want to know if he's meeting alone with a woman and when the meeting should be over. If he's going to make stops on the way home, I want to know how long they are going to take, so I won't worry that he's meeting the woman he had the affair with. If

29

he cooperates, I can trust him. He's pretty understanding about my need to know.

Jennifer's husband, Tom, had several affairs before they
were married four years ago. Jennifer uses a more secretive
technique to monitor his activities.

Tom told me about his affairs before we were married. I believed he was genuinely repentant and that
it would never happen again. But a year after we were
married, I found several pornographic magazines in
the back of his closet when I was cleaning one day.
Now I feel paranoid with fear and worry that he's back
to his old habits. I know it's probably wrong, but I frequently check up on him when he's away from home.
I've even paid people he doesn't know to help me so
he won't find out. It's crazy, I know, but I can't seem
to stop. I'm so afraid of being hurt.

When a woman's partner is involved in sexual addiction,
she battles a dragon she can never slay. No matter how hard
she tries to control him, no matter how hard she tries to be
the perfect wife, no matter how attractive or slender she
keeps herself, no matter how sexually available she is, she
cannot provide him with the one thing he seeks—another
woman. She is powerless to keep his mind on her.

Codependent Response

The sex addict who marries doesn't usually know it, but
rarely is his choice made through random attraction. Just
the opposite. His instincts lead him to select a woman who
will help take care of him—a codependent woman who fears
abandonment and looks to others to validate her self-worth.
A cycle is manifested within their marriage; she becomes a
co-addict, a person who is addicted to him to the point of

not leaving, even when his sexual sin jeopardizes their marriage, their children, and possibly her health through the threat of sexually transmitted diseases, including HIV. She believes that somehow if she could *be* more, *do* more, *pray* more, and *trust* long enough or hard enough, he would be satisfied and stay home. She feels as if she hasn't given God enough time yet. She views the slightest variation in his behavior as a sign that her partner is finally changing, or she lives on the prayer that tomorrow will be different.

"He has become her barometer, her radar, her emotional gauge," explains Robin Norwood, author of *Women Who Love Too Much.*

> And she watches him constantly. All her feelings are generated by his behavior. At the time that she gives him the power to rock and sway her emotionally, she runs interference between him and the world. She tries to make him look better than he is and to make them as a couple appear happier than they are. She rationalizes away his every failure, her every disappointment, and while she hides the truth from the world she also hides it from herself. Unable to accept that he is what he is, and that his problems are his, not hers, she experiences a profound sense of having failed in all her energetic attempts to change him.[8]

Christian marriage counselor Mark Luciano goes on to say:

> The intermeshing of traits that creates this downward spiral in marriage is what is commonly called codependency. A simple definition of codependency is the tendency to take the responsibilities of another as your own. In a troubled marriage, codependency is the tendency to take your spouse's responsibility to work on his or her character defect as your responsibility. Not only will codependency not cause your spouse to change, it will destroy your marriage.[9]

Does your husband or significant other have a pattern of affairs, pornography, lust—or do you suspect he does? Do you tell yourself that if he really loved you, he would change? Do you believe, despite all evidence to the contrary, that things will somehow improve? Do you blame yourself for not having tried hard enough to please him? Do you make excuses for his behavior? Do you believe that if you could only get his current girlfriend out of his life, then all your problems would be over?

If you answer "yes" to several of these questions, you are probably caught in the snare of codependent behavior—behavior that actually interferes with your husband becoming willing to change.

What Are the Steps to Gain Freedom?

There are steps we can take to gain freedom. They are not easy, however, and they require commitment to an ongoing process in our own lives. This process will take time. It also demands rigorous honesty and growth on our part, but it can free us from the fear, worry, guilt, and spiritual decay that lurks within codependency.

Admit It Happens

If we are to deal with this problem in our marriages and homes, admitting it happens presents the first step toward healing and growth. Only when we *admit* it happens can we take the necessary second step and *accept* that it happens, which frees us to take the most important step and *adapt* to his behavior proactively.

Melody Beattie writes in *Codependent No More,* "Facing and coming to terms with *what is*—is a beneficial act. Acceptance brings peace. It is frequently the turning point for change."[10] We can't adapt to a problem until we accept that it exists. There is an important difference between acknowledgment and acceptance, however. Acknowledgment is admitting, being able to say that something is true. Acceptance goes much deeper. Acceptance doesn't mean yielding or giving up or tolerating; acceptance means receiving on an emotional level what one admits to be true on an intellectual level. In the case of an unfaithful husband, it means giving up our denial and accepting that he has a serious problem, and that by association, we have a serious problem, too.

Detach

We will remain painfully trapped in feelings of powerlessness until we choose to detach from our husband's behavior and recognize that his sexual sin is *his*, not ours. Dr. Jennifer Schneider says, "Detachment is a much misunderstood concept. It does not mean we do not care or we are washing our hands of the person. It means we recognize that we cannot solve another person's problems for him, and worrying about the situation will not bring about change. Learning to detach allows us to love without going crazy."[11]

Mark Luciano goes on to explain:

Detachment from that which is beyond your control is the all-important attitude that differentiates between what you are responsible for and what you are not, what you have the power to control and what you do not. Likewise, detachment maintains the line between care or concern for what another person has done and "butting in."

At first, detachment may sound insensitive. Detachment is not indifference. It requires a real commitment to yourself and to the person involved. Accepting full responsibility for yourself implies you will act to the best of your ability in any given situation and refrain from controlling the other person's decisions, emotions, or actions. It actually frees you to give yourself more effectively, and therefore more lovingly, in relationships.[12]

That means letting go of control, anger, and possibly even the man himself if he chooses not to stay. Robin Norwood poignantly describes how this "letting go" can feel.

In taking these steps, you will be required to do something from time to time that is very difficult. You will have to face the terrible emptiness within that surfaces when you are not focused on someone else. Sometimes the emptiness will be so deep, you will almost be able to feel the wind blowing through the place where your heart should be. Allow yourself to feel it, in all its intensity, otherwise you'll look for another unhealthy way to distract yourself. Embrace the emptiness and know that you will not always feel this way.[13]

Accept Our Powerlessness to Control

Experiencing completely our own powerlessness allows us to truly let go of our husbands, our families, and our own lives and *really* turn everything over to God. We are not letting go into a void; God is there waiting to carry the burden and responsibility for us. There is a beautiful prayer often found in Twelve Step circles that I have found helpful. For me, the Serenity Prayer provides a calming, centering reminder that I'm not fighting my battles alone. Over and over again, its simple message reminds me that God is here beside me. It says, "God, grant me the serenity to accept the things I cannot change, the courage to change the things I can, and the wisdom to know the difference."

The Old Testament Book of Isaiah contains one of those wonderful promises of God that we can claim during times of adversity. Originally given as a promise to deliver the children of Israel from their captivity in Babylon, the passage from Isaiah 43 goes on to say that this promise is extended to "everyone who is called by my name" (v. 7).

Here is God's personal promise to you as you walk through the painful days ahead:

> Do not fear, for I have redeemed you;
> I have called you by name; you are Mine!
> When you pass through the waters, I will be with you;
> And through the rivers, they will not overflow you.
> When you walk through the fire, you will not be scorched,
> Nor will the flame burn you.
> For I am the LORD your God . . .
> Since you are honored and I love you.
>
> Isaiah 43:1–4 NASB

When we surrender our husbands into God's hands, we become willing to take all the risks this step involves. Only then can we move on to the one thing we can change—ourselves.

2

The Power of Healing Connections

Dropping Your Mask, Revealing Your Pain

> Two are better than one,
> because they have a good return for their work:
> If one falls down, his friend can help him up.
> *Ecclesiastes 4:9–10 NIV*

Back in the United States from their honeymoon in France, Dick and Julie pulled into the driveway as husband and wife for the first time. Julie had looked forward to being carried over the threshold when this day finally arrived, but today that didn't seem appropriate. Without a word, they got out of the car. Julie unlocked the front door and entered their home in this Rocky Mountain town where Dick had been called to serve as assistant pastor. Everything looked the same. The furniture they had lovingly selected together and set up before the wedding invited her into the cozy living room, just the way she remembered it. And the jagged ridges and peaks of the nearby Rockies still etched the sky with their ragged edges and filled the vista beyond the living room window. They sat there, anchoring the world, as if time changed nothing.

But something had changed. The pain and loneliness she felt proved it. Slowly she followed Dick up the stairs as he carried their luggage to the bedroom; pictures of their long but happy courtship, Dick's seminary degree, and mementos from their summer mission trip to Asia were still where they'd placed them. The photos all said that her husband was a wonderful Christian man who cared about other people. But this week she had also learned something else about him.

I've got to get out of here, Julie thought. *I'll go get groceries.* Knowing she planned to go to the Christian bookstore as well, she told Dick she needed to shop to fill the refrigerator and left.

In town, Julie pushed open the glass door and stepped into the Christian bookstore. *Oh, it feels good,* she thought as the gentle strains of "Amazing Grace" welcomed her. *Where should I look?* she wondered. *Maybe in the section labeled Recovery, the one on Marriage, and possibly Men's Issues.* Walking down the rows of books, she ran her finger slowly across the top of the spines, scanning for titles that might help her understand the last twenty-four hours. She pulled out *Addicted to Love* by Steve Arterburn and grasped it hopefully. Continuing to search, she was rewarded with *Faithful and True* by Mark Laaser.

After lighting a fire that night, Julie sat down and began to read. She learned that lust frequently lurks just beyond the edge of the male mind, a tempter and tormentor with whom many Christian men do daily spiritual battle. She also began to understand that the things that happen to a man—especially in childhood but also in adult life—often provide the arsenal to which Satan returns to seize the weapons of his warfare.

A year later, after Julie and Dick moved to Seattle, Julie and I began meeting in an intensive mentoring relationship. Now Julie is asking God to help her understand the male mind—as much as a woman ever can. She still wants Dick to change, but she's learning to channel her energy into changing the only person she can—herself.

Like Julie, it hurts most women to know that on our broken planet our husbands sometimes feel attracted to other women. And whether our husbands merely fight frequent temptation or are deeply ensnared in sexual addiction, we long for help to understand what the man we love thinks and feels at those times. Why is it happening? Why does he do this? Often we don't know where to turn. Help is available in several forms: books, counseling, seminars and workshops, and most helpful of all, peer-led support groups. Through these tools, I now understand (and seek to help other women understand) that when a man struggles with lust, his thoughts and behavior aren't really about his wife. I've learned that no matter how good a woman looks or how sexy she tries to be, it is the man's own issues that fuel his problem. But this knowledge alone doesn't ease the pain we feel, and experts tell us this pain often leaves deep wounds.

A woman named Shawna called me yesterday after our *Love Under Fire* radio show. She told me that she still lacks a nurturing group to help her heal. Her husband had an affair, and she poignantly described her situation this way:

> I don't know what to do. I can't seem to pull myself together; I'm so flooded by my hurt and anger. I feel so alone. My husband won't let me talk about my feelings and we left our church because of the embarrassment. There is one woman who has stood by me

but I can't lean on her every day. I really need someone's help. Can you tell me where to turn?

A report titled *How Connections Heal* explains that the
"disconnections" that occur when there is a painful break
in a deep relationship such as a marriage "lead to psycho-
logical wounds, especially when the relational environment
is unresponsive."[1] In other words, when a husband's actions
have hurt us and he doesn't care or doesn't want to talk
about it, like Shawna's husband, deep hurt takes place
inside us. The authors go on to explain that this often cre-
ates an inability to help yourself and reach out to others
for help and support. We experience damage to our "sense
of self-worth, a decrease in energy, and finally, and perhaps most importantly, a confusing sense of isolation in
which the person feels locked out of the possibility of real
connection."[2]

How can these wounds be healed? There is one important principle professionals agree on: We need others; we
shouldn't remain in isolation.

Benefits of a Support Group

Dr. Jennifer Schneider, author of the wonderfully helpful book, *Back from Betrayal*, believes that "recovery is best
accomplished through a combination of counseling and
attendance at peer group support meetings."[3] Gentle guidance by a good counselor can lead us into a new place where
we begin to understand and accept our husbands for who
they are—men with feet of clay—then guide us through
the work needed to heal our wounded egos and assist us
in rebuilding healthy self-esteem. If you can possibly find
and afford a good counselor, by all means do so. But individual counseling is expensive and simply not an option
for many of us.

Learning from Other Women

I have found that talking to other women often helps the most. I continue to learn from those who tell me their painful stories, but perhaps the greatest healing and growth occurs when we join other women in a support group. Here we form bonds and gain understanding and healing that's not available from any other source. As we listen to other women share, we also begin to learn important new lessons. We learn that no matter how hard we push or endeavor to control, we are totally powerless over our husbands' behavior. And we begin to see more clearly that our self-esteem does not need to depend on him or anyone else. Perhaps most importantly, we learn that it is appropriate to set limits—based on principles from God's Word—on what is acceptable behavior for us within the marriage relationship. Melinda feels grateful that she learned these lessons from a handful of loving supporters. She shared her story with me during a pain-filled phone call.

> The pastor of the church we attended didn't know how to help me with my feelings after I discovered Greg used pornography. I felt devastated and unable to cope, and very, very alone. And then I found a handful of women to meet with and talk to—women who were honest. It took other women letting me vent and not condemning me. It took other women being honest with me, too, about the things going on in their own lives. I never found a "safe" person until I found this special group.
>
> After a while, I was able to separate my worth from Greg's addiction; I began to see that what he did didn't reflect on me or my value as a woman. It was about his own broken places, not mine. I finally came to realize that his involvement with pornography amounted to breaking our wedding vow, and as I grew, I became

strong enough to confront his behavior. I set limits on
what I thought was appropriate behavior within our
marriage and what I believed wasn't. He could either
meet those limits by being mentally faithful or leave.

It is important that as we think through what behaviors
are outside our tolerance that we check any demeaning, critical spirit we find within. A man will perceive an unkind
spirit, and it will only interfere with our efforts to save the
marriage and pollute our own spiritual health. Meanness
isn't our goal but rather a calm, firm, steadfast spirit that
knows we're right.

The emotional and spiritual turmoil we go through as
we work on our own issues is draining. As we grow and
begin to wrench our focus away from our husbands'
thoughts and actions, we experience a void—a big hole that
only God and supportive understanding can fill. And the
acceptance and understanding we receive from other
women in a support group setting provides powerful healing properties that help plug that hole.

A Remedy for Aloneness within the Church

Sadly, a feeling of "aloneness" is often stronger for Christian women than it is for those outside the church. The
shame associated with sexual sin, the judging, and the
absence of real grace lead most women to clutch their family secrets tightly to their chests, lest anyone find out.
Recently a woman named Marie called and asked if we
could talk. She told me how she feels at her church.

We've been pillars in our church. We led the youth
group, served in leadership, and have been looked up
to as the perfect Christian family. But since I found out
about my husband's secret addiction to pornography
and his three affairs, we play a game. When we go to

41

> church I put on my happy mask and nice clothes, and
> when people ask how I am I always answer, "Oh, fine,"
> but inside I'm dying. I don't know how much longer I
> can hang on.

Marie is not alone in her charade. Few of the women—or men—who talk to us have ventured out from behind their masks in complete honesty with even one other Christian friend. Some don't even want to use their real names when they talk to us on the phone, their fear and shame runs so deep.

Allowing ourselves to become emotionally vulnerable frightens us. To cover our fear, we create a slick surface of spiritual maturity and we hide our pain—and ourselves—behind our masks. But spiritual growth becomes stunted when we cut off and deny our emotional needs, and it becomes virtually impossible to maintain healthy self-esteem.

The fear that others will discover the family secret keeps many people from getting the help that could salvage their lives and their relationships. In a good support group, your presence there and what is discussed never leaves the group. Your privacy is respected and protected. Because each participant risks honesty, each one values the shared need for confidentiality. James 5:16 tells us to practice this kind of honest sharing when it says, "Confess your sins to one another, and pray for one another, so that you may be healed" (NASB). And in Galatians 6:2, we're encouraged to "Bear one another's burdens, and thus fulfill the law of Christ" (NASB). God wants us to leave our lonely caves of isolation and help each other bear life's burdens.

I'll never forget Connie, a woman in a support group I led in a local church several years ago. From all outward appearances, Connie had it all together. About fifty, she had a beautiful home, a terrific marriage, and great kids. She also actively served in her church. Over the weeks as the group bonded, those of us around the circle began to develop trust and true love for one another. Each of us cautiously pulled back a corner of our masks an inch at a time, revealing deeper and deeper personal truths—each one but Connie. I wondered why until she called me at home one night after our support group meeting. Her voice choking with tears, she said, "Marsha, I want to share in our group. I really need to share, but I'm terrified. I just can't." As I gently asked her why, she told me about the childhood hurts she still carried and covered behind a restricting fifty-year-old mask—hurts she couldn't seem to muster the courage to risk and share, even with Christian friends. Connie never came back to the group after that night. She dropped out never knowing that she had finally found a safe place to unveil her fears and to dissolve them.

Ann found a safe place when, over several months, she slowly began to share with one other woman about the seismic shocks rumbling through her marriage. I asked Ann how it felt to wear a mask and then begin to slowly come out from behind it.

> I've always felt there were so many things I needed to hide from other Christians. Randy's use of pornography was just one of many. I felt that I was the protector of his image. Most of the friendships I had at that time within the church were couple friendships. I felt that if I told the female in a relationship, she would become uncomfortable around my husband, and we'd lose those friendships.
>
> I also felt shame—shame for Randy and for myself. If I told anyone, I would be admitting that my husband was living in sin and had not gotten victory over it. I think I also thought that no other Christian men struggle with pornography like my husband did, so other women wouldn't understand or be supportive.
>
> After being married for about ten years, I met a woman at church who exhibited a refreshing kind of honesty. I found out that she was searching and strug-

gling just like I was. I found out that her marriage wasn't perfect, either, and that she had recently discovered that her husband had an affair during their engagement. In time I was able to share with that dear friend what was going on in my own marriage.

Looking back, I see that she earned my trust by being real. I could tell her anything and know that she wouldn't reject me or Randy. She saw all of us as people in process. What a gift! That was the beginning of my gaining the courage, with the help of a support group, to confront Randy's addiction, and God used that confrontation to begin to change Randy.

For Ann, finding just one other safe person was the beginning of eventual freedom from the sin trap in her marriage. But a support group is more than a place to share our hurt and pain. If we desire true spiritual growth, we must also bring with us into the group the willingness for God to change *us*. And because it is also a place to chisel away at our own character defects, what lies ahead involves hard work and commitment.

Facing Our Own Broken Places

If we hope to turn our scrutinizing gaze away from our husbands' inner landscape and penetratingly peer into the desert of our own souls, we need to use this support group to remove our masks and become vulnerably honest. For when we are totally honest, most of us must admit that our codependent obsession with our *husband's* character defects has fostered an addiction of our own—always wondering what's going through his mind when he passes an attractive woman, always resenting the alluring female forms that beckon him from the magazine covers by the grocery checkout, always wondering what he says and does around the women at work.

When we try to stop these obsessive thoughts, a nearly overwhelming anxiety rushes in to replace our dependence on watching and worrying about our husbands' thoughts and behavior. After all, if *we* don't control them, who will? During this lonely, anxious time, we must have support, reassurance, and understanding constantly available in person or by phone. Only women who walk the same path—women who are either fighting the same obsessions or those who've already fought and won—can truly understand the painful withdrawal we feel when we give up trying to monitor our husbands.

A Safe Environment

When we find a good support group, we've finally found a safe environment to talk openly and honestly about our past and present problems. We've discovered a protected harbor where we can share all our feelings and experiences, no matter how ugly they sound or appear. In a healthy group we don't attempt to "fix" each other, nor do we interrupt when someone else shares. This means that we consider sacred our responsibility to listen to others without offering opinions or sermons. No one should say, "You're a Christian. You just need to focus on the Word and pray more!"

The knowledge that these women will respect our need for privacy and will keep confidential our deepest confessions ensures us that we can reveal our worst secrets without having them repeated. And when we hear others share their secrets, we realize we aren't alone in our dysfunctional behaviors. It's liberating to listen to others share deeply. Their stories stimulate our own conscience and we recognize ourselves in their histories. We begin to remember what we've forgotten or blocked from our own surface memory, and events and feelings from the past seep like oil to the surface of our minds. We learn more about ourselves—both our strengths and our weaknesses.

As we recognize the similarities in our struggles, we find the courage to penetrate the dark alleys within our own souls and confront and confess what lurks there in the shadows. But perhaps our greatest liberation comes when we find ourselves extending grace to others in spite of their flaws and their secrets. Our model in this ministry of grace-giving is Jesus himself. In Romans 15:7 we're challenged to "accept one another, just as Christ also accepted us to the glory of God" (NASB). Embracing others in this way helps us with the crucial step of extending that grace *to ourselves*. This is the beginning of self-acceptance, the beginning of the death of shame, that death so necessary to take healthy responsibility for our own sin and guilt and move into God's healing forgiveness.

Learning to Trust and Share Honestly

It may take time before you feel enough trust to share your secrets. If that's true, talk honestly about your lack of trust. As you do, and aren't rejected, your trust will begin to grow. In time it will feel safe enough to slowly peel back your mask; you will become less secretive and eventually feel a secure sense of belonging. Your inner isolation will lift like an early morning mist, and you will feel understood and accepted.

As we tear down our protective walls, we form sisterly bonds with the women in our group, because we let them know us in a way few people have known us before. Even though at first you may feel uncomfortable with the raw honesty in a healthy support group, after a while, you will probably find it feels so refreshing that you become "hooked" on it—not because of its melodrama but because it produces healing. You will feel yourself growing as God works in your life through your courageous honesty and self-disclosure. You will sense new character replacing old behaviors and sinful patterns. This is the "renewing of your mind" that Paul tells us to expect in Romans 12:2 (NIV). And it all begins with finding the courage to be honest.

Finding a Support Group

Finding a support group won't be easy; in fact, it will probably require much effort. It's even possible that you'll need to start your own group. Appendix 1 tells you how to do this and gives you guidance you can follow step-by-step.

Finding a group may present an extra dilemma for women in church leadership. Having grown up in a minister's home, I know that those in leadership often feel it's unwise to reveal family problems to the people among whom they minister. If you simply can't feel comfortable with deep self-disclosure among these women, I recommend that you start your own group composed of pastors' wives and other women in leadership or that you attend a group in a neighboring city. But don't let your position prevent you from reaching out for help. That humbling step will open the door to a whole new level of personal freedom and spiritual growth.

The Group's Focus

Ideally, when we're caught in the cross fire from our husband's secret war, we need a support group that helps us deal with our swirling emotions and put a stop to our obsessive reacting, monitoring, controlling. In short, we need a place to learn to quit trying to change *him*. Although some women can deal with these issues in a good Al-Anon group, in Al-Anon the primary focus is codependent reactions to a spouse's drinking, as opposed to his sexual behaviors. But if nothing else is available and you can't start your own group, these groups may be helpful for you. To find an Al-Anon support group in your area, call the Alcoholics Anonymous number in the phone book for information.

Whichever group you ultimately choose, choose a group for women only. Not only do other women better understand our feelings, experiences, and issues, but with no men present we also avoid the temptation to continue our unhealthy dependency on yet another man.

To better understand what we're looking for, we need to understand what a support group is not. In their book, *Creating Safe Places,* Curt Grayson and Jan Johnson tell us that a good support group is not

a Bible study
group therapy
a gripe session, though hurts are shared
a screaming session, though anger is often expressed
a rehashing of the past, though past events may be
   related
an emotional scene, though some members may cry
   and hug[4]

If in a group we hear others recounting long stories with lots of "he said . . . and then I said . . ." in them, we are probably in the wrong group. Remember we need to share our hurts and pain, but we also need to be honest about ourselves and work on our own weaknesses. In addition to understanding, there should also be a side to the group that helps us take responsibility for our own behavior.

When we do find or start a group, we need to make a strong commitment to ourselves and to the group if we want to benefit. Expect it to take some time to feel completely comfortable; relationships that run deep require shared time and experience to develop. It may also take a while to learn the jargon if it exists and to grasp the group process. Different groups will have different characteristics, though the basic format from group to group is usually the same.

Complete Acceptance at Last

Your efforts in finding a group will provide something you may never have had before: a safe place to talk honestly, to trust completely, and to feel your pain at its deepest level so that you can heal and work on your own codependency and character defects. You will also gain the courage to confront your husband about his behavior if that's something you can't do yet.

In her beautiful poem "Your Gifts," Christian author and therapist Juanita Ryan expresses the treasure we find in true friendships, such as those found in a good support group.

Your Gifts

You hold out gifts to me,
Generous offerings
of your heart.

With one hand you give
the gift of trusting me
with the sorrows and longings
and wonder that is you.
A gift
brown wrapped in courage
and humility.

With the other hand you give
the gift of tireless interest in me,
breaking into smiles at my growth,
caressing my wounds with your voice.
A gift
gold wrapped in gentleness
and respect.
Your gifts
are rare treasures.
You give me you.
You give me me.

The gifts of healing and encouragement can be yours as well. It all begins when you find the courage to reach out and ask for help.

3

The Curse
of Codependency

Trading Yourself for Love

> Codependency holds a person hostage to other peo-
> ple's behaviors, moods, or opinions, and the codepen-
> dent bases his or her worth and actions on someone
> else's life. It's a terrible bondage.
>
> *Nancy Groom,*
> *From Bondage to Bonding*

The lamp beside the sofa in the tucked away hospital waiting room where we had been meeting cast a warm glow over Tanya's curly red hair. Knees tucked up beside her, Tanya hugged a blue throw pillow with one hand and wiped the charcoal-colored rivulets across her cheeks with the other. She was a grown woman, but she was feeling the pain she experienced as a child. Tanya's father habitually ignored her, and she never felt good enough or pretty enough or smart enough to merit his attention.

If only I were prettier, I wouldn't feel like Ray is always looking at the sexy girls in bikinis at the beach. I hate

> going there on Saturdays. I just can't quit wondering
> what's going through his mind. I especially hate it when
> we walk past a tall blonde with legs up to here. And I
> hate it when he flirts with other women.

I first met Tanya while doing a seminar in another state. She told me her jealousy and character defects were seriously damaging her marriage, but she didn't know how to stop. She asked if we could begin a mentoring process over the phone and through the mail, and I agreed to give it a try. Each week as we talked, Tanya tried to focus on changing herself and letting God change Ray if he needed changing. But she wasn't having much success. Her obsession with her husband's behavior always returned. She wasn't yet ready to accept that she is powerless to change Ray and that the only person she can change is Tanya.

Admitting We Are Powerless to Change Our Husbands

I know firsthand how hard it is to keep our eyes off a husband's behavior, because it's a monumental struggle for me, too. But the reality is that no amount of energy, no magic formula—nothing will bring about true change in another person. However, if we take the same energy and apply it to ourselves, God can do great things in our lives.

First we have to really "get it"—down in our heart of hearts—*we are powerless to change our husbands*. In his classic book, *If Only You Would Change,* Christian marriage counselor Mark Luciano tells us "you have to admit that you cannot manage your marriage problems by yourself. This means that you recognize the futility of your attempts to change your spouse."[1]

Put simply, we must admit that the strategies we have used to change our husbands have not worked and that every attempt to change or control them will ultimately fail. Admitting we are powerless requires surrendering our husbands and our lives *completely* to God. It requires accepting that this is our reality. This doesn't sound like much of a solution, but it is the only solution that will calm our screaming fears and bring peace to our troubled hearts. We must surrender the obsession to try to change our spouses because it is this obsession that blocks our emotional, intellectual, and spiritual growth.

Two or three years had passed since I first read Mark Luciano's book before I really understood what powerlessness means. It wasn't like a light being switched on in my head when I finally got it; it was more like steeping my soul in the reality of that truth. Yet even now, sometimes my anxieties get the best of me. Occasionally I still obsess about what Pat is doing, especially when he's late getting home. At those times I have to resurrender my marriage and my life to God, releasing everything to his love and care. It helps if I hold my hands out in front of me and open my palms, symbolically letting go heavenward once more. But then what? Luciano provides some guidance.

> The obsessive searchlight trained on your spouse will be refocused to look at what is within your power to change, namely yourself. The energy spent worrying and fretting over what your spouse will do next is more effectively used to fulfill your own needs. As you implement each new step, you will find you have recovered more and more of your life's energy.[2]

Facing Our Own Codependency

I believe that for those of us whose husbands struggle with sexual temptations, change requires addressing our own codependency, self-esteem, and character defects. Ultimately, we need to ask God to help us see our own character defects and help us change them.

As Christians, we often feel confused by the codependency concept. Jesus taught us to care for and about other people. He said, "Love your enemies, do good to those who hate you, bless those who curse you, pray for those who mistreat you" (Luke 6:27–28 NASB). The Epistles teach us to bear one another's burdens and to sacrifice for others. Does that mean that codependency is spiritual? Was Jesus codependent? I don't believe so. The Gospels show us a Jesus who wasn't afraid to say no, to speak the truth when he saw sinful behavior, and to take time out by himself and with friends. Jesus modeled a balanced way to live in relationships—he cared for others *and* he cared for himself.

Nancy Groom says, "At the heart of codependent living is an arrogant and fear-based refusal to rely solely on God, an unwillingness to rest in His grace, to be satisfied with His provision and to set our hearts on obedience. Codependency is not just unhelpful but dreadfully and crucially wrong."[3]

An author who fights her own battle with codependency, Nancy Groom is the wife of a recovering alcoholic. She goes on to describe a codependent person this way:

> A codependent person is "addicted," not to a destructive substance, but a destructive pattern of relating to other people, a pattern usually learned in childhood. . . . Codependency *holds a person hostage* to other people's behaviors, moods, or opinions, and the codependent bases his or her worth and action on someone else's life. It's a terrible bondage.[4]

Childlike neediness is one form this bondage takes.

Childlike Neediness

I experienced this sort of neediness again last week after Pat had been especially preoccupied with his work for a couple of days. Lying in bed beside him that night, I felt desperate for reassurance of his love. I wasn't really dreaming, because I wasn't asleep, but I wasn't totally awake, either.

Somehow, in that in-between time of being neither awake nor asleep, I had reverted to feeling like the little girl I was so long ago. In reality I was lying in bed beside Pat. Emotionally, I was in a dark dungeon, alone and terrified. I could almost feel myself running my hands over the cold gray slabs, searching for a way out of my prison.

Sounds silly, doesn't it? But it didn't feel silly at the time. The scared little girl who still resides in a tiny part of me doesn't take over very often anymore, but I had taken my eyes off my heavenly Father and watched my earthly husband instead, and my old codependent personality traits were quick to cut in. The neediness of a child is one trait often exhibited by codependents. "But how," you might ask, "can a grown woman feel and act like a little girl who needs someone to take care of her?" I remember well one experience that provided the soil in which this trait began to grow in me.

When I was six, my parents, who were new Christians, felt called to ministry. So they bundled up our family and belongings, and we moved from Washington State to the San Francisco Bay area, where Dad attended Bible college. Those were challenging years, financially and physically. My mother became gravely ill on several occasions, and once she was so sick that I was sent back to Washington, along with my younger sister and two little brothers, to live with family members for a while. We were with people who loved us, and there really was nothing else Mom and Dad could do, but nonetheless, I missed them terribly, hated going to a new school temporarily, and worried that we'd never be together again. I guess I wasn't emotionally strong enough to deal with the situation appropriately, because I've battled an eight-year-old's fear of abandonment through all the years that have come and gone since then. Nancy Groom writes about these kinds of fears.

> Children learn to depend on themselves and on others in terribly wrong ways. Soul wounds do not heal if they are ignored.

They continue to shape and govern our emotions, our self-images, and our ways of interacting in relationships, long beyond the childhood in which they were received. It is not uncommon for codependents to suddenly wonder what's going on when something happens and their reaction is out of proportion to the surface significance of the incident. Perhaps they are living in a different time zone, thrown back emotionally into a childhood situation they felt unable to handle then and thus feel unable to handle as adults as well. The resources codependents use to manage their lives and relationships as adults have been conditioned by the ways they adapted to . . . their childhoods.[5]

Adrianne sometimes expresses childlike neediness, too. She frequently talks about the gaping hole left in her heart since her early years.

> My dad never showed me any love. Even now, when I try to talk to him he isn't interested. I've wanted his love and attention all my life. All I want is a daddy who believes I'm special, and shows me how much he loves me.

Since she can't get her need met by her father, Adrianne attempts to get it from her husband. But Damon doesn't want to be needed like a daddy. He wants an adult wife with whom he can be an equal. In our present attempts to meet past needs, we only drive our husbands away. A needy, codependent woman desperately wants someone else to be there for her; she needs someone to rescue her from her loneliness and isolation. She expects this other person to make up for what's missing in her interior, to feed her emotional hunger and quench her thirsting soul.

When we believe that our needs aren't being met and that our husbands could meet them if they were willing and really loved us, we fuel the obsessive flame that we direct at our spouses. Serenity finally comes when we believe our needs will be met by our heavenly Father, no matter what our husbands do. We can also draw strength and courage by bonding with other women who are committed to growth.

I am finally learning to take these steps, though I still slip at times. The woman I've become can usually soothe the troubled child within and reassure her that together, God and I can deal with life and whatever new situation or experience may wait around the next bend.

Control at Any Cost

Codependency can also manifest itself in the desire to control situations by holding things together, no matter what the consequences. A book of fear serves as our codependency operations manual. The rules in this manual instruct us to control our environment lest our safety, finances, and family reputation be destroyed by our husbands. But where is faith? What do we do with God? Fear cancels out faith, and control blocks the power of our prayers. Some women even allow themselves and their children to live in horrible circumstances rather than relinquish control and risk other people finding out their dreadful family secret. Janine, a Christian woman in the Seattle area who called after one of our radio broadcasts, provides a prime example.

> For the last eighteen years my husband has been addicted to sex and pornography. And for fourteen of those years, he's been HIV positive. We don't have sex for obvious reasons, and he uses pornography— both magazines and the Internet—in its place. Even though I know I shouldn't stay in this marriage and expose my children to this situation, I can't leave. Everyone would know. And besides, I don't want my children raised in a single family home. That's the way I was raised.

Women like Janine often learn this control style of coping early in life. Most likely, Janine helped hold her broken childhood family together as well.

Helen also controls by staying in the mess her husband has made of their life. Because he's in Christian leadership, letting go in faith could carry an enormous price tag.

> My husband was a pastor and we've been married for twenty-six years. He started having the affairs that I'm aware of about nineteen years ago. He finally quit pastoring because it was too hard to keep people from seeing his behavior. He flirts with women everywhere we go—the grocery store, at friends' homes, even at church when we attend together. He's an evangelist now, so he's on the road a lot and his reputation doesn't follow him so closely. I'm miserable; I've let myself go physically, but I'm terrified of financial ruin if I leave.

Releasing control of her husband's secret could cost Helen dearly. Her financial security depends on his evangelistic ministry. Because her husband is known widely, lost friendships and lost ministry support could cut to the core of Helen's life. As author Nancy Groom says, "These are high stakes, and somehow caretaking, even if it's patronizing, seems a more attractive alternative. Why stop the warning and crisis prevention and managing and emotional coddling if the consequences can be so dire? Isn't a codependent's control preferable to disaster?"[6]

Relational Isolation

Janine and Helen, like most of the women we hear from, are living in a form of emotional isolation, bound to an unspoken code of secrecy about their husbands' behavior. To confront that behavior and let others know the truth would mean admitting that their lives are out of control and that they can't manage effectively. So instead, they wear masks to project the illusion of "normalcy." Everything seems to depend on it. Because they wear masks, co-dependent people live in relational isolation; not only will they not let anyone know their secret, they will never again *need* anyone. I remember with cold clarity the day I made this vow in my first marriage.

Years ago my life looked very different than it does now. Married at eighteen, a mother at twenty, I soon found myself in a troubled relationship. I reacted with classic co-dependence. I blamed my husband for all the painful circumstances in our relationship and life and let my anger spill out on those around me. For years I prayed for what I thought was God's will to be done in my husband's life. When God didn't see fit to listen or to act in accordance to my timetable, I tried control and manipulation. But that only made things worse.

Finally, spiritually spent and emotionally wrung out, I silently declared emotional independence. My declaration felt almost ceremonial. Standing in my family room in northern California, I decided to purposely freeze my innermost self so hard and so cold that nothing could ever hurt me again. I didn't mean to lock God out of the deep freeze that iced my insides; I meant to leave the door ajar for him. But God cannot warm a subzero heart. Without meaning to, I had frozen God out. I've learned that I'm not the only one to react this way.

Many women determine to make it on their own, to chart their own course through the sea of life without ever having to ask anyone for help. Hurt, angry, and wounded, they've decided, *Never again. Never will I turn the controls over to anyone else.* Without realizing it, their hardened heart says, *I don't need God; I don't need love. I can navigate life's seas on my own.*

When we determine to never let our guard down to anyone again, we refuse to look to other people to meet the deep longings in our hearts. Naturally, it would be unwise to base our emotional stability on the belief that no one will ever let us down. People are human, after all. While we need to stop letting other people's opinions and behaviors form the foundation of our stability and worth, we *were* created to crave relationship. God created Eve because Adam felt lonely. Both in the garden and outside, they shared mutual interdependence—each needed the other.

Relationships come with no guarantees that our deepest longings for love and acceptance will be met. In fact, because we live on a fallen planet, we can count on disappointment. Mutual interdependence is challenging at best; at worst, it remains unavailable or incredibly painful. But to love is to risk. C. S. Lewis described this dilemma beautifully.

> To love at all is to be vulnerable. Love anything, and your heart will certainly be wrung and possibly be broken. If you want to make sure of keeping it intact, you must give your heart to no one, not even to an animal. Wrap it carefully round with hobbies and little luxuries, avoid all entanglements, lock it up safe in the casket or coffin of your selfishness. But in that casket—safe, dark, motionless, airless—it will change. It will not be broken; it will become unbreakable, impenetrable, irredeemable. The alternative to tragedy, or at least to the risk of tragedy, is damnation. The only place outside Heaven where you can be perfectly safe from all the dangers and perturbations of love is Hell.[7]

Would we really rather lock our hearts in a safe, dark, airless coffin than take the risks that loving demands? Nancy Groom has said it well. "There's no way around it," she says. "If I'm going to love and be loved, I'm going to be hurt and uncomfortable. Only grace affords the courage necessary to take the risks."[8]

God's Power Is Ready and Available

We can't make our husbands' character defects and addiction go away with any of our codependent methods. However, God's power stands ready and available to help us deal with our problems but only if we acknowledge them honestly. When we cover, control, caretake, isolate, or declare total emotional independence, we shackle ourselves in the chains of our own fear.

Second Timothy 1:7 reminds us that "God hath not given us the spirit of fear; but of power, and of love, and of a sound mind" (KJV). We'll need large doses of all three as we prepare to confront our husbands' unhealthy behavior. If we'll only trust God to take care of us, we can appropriate his power and love.

Another of Juanita Ryan's poems models the balance we need if we hope to deal with our feelings and others' behaviors in healthy, helpful ways—a balance that can only be gained by trusting God.

Give Me Grace

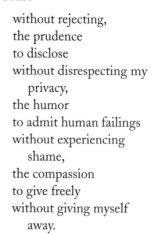

Give me the grace
to care
without neglecting my
    needs,
the humility
to assist
without rescuing,
the kindness
to be clear
without being cold,
the mercy
to be angry
without rejecting,
the prudence
to disclose
without disrespecting my
    privacy,
the humor
to admit human failings
without experiencing
    shame,
the compassion
to give freely
without giving myself
    away.

— 4 —

Caring Enough to Confront

An Early Blowout or Slow Leak?

It is only when he sees everything of value to him—
his home, his children, his wife, his reputation—begin
to slip away that his choices will become clear. . . .
What I'm saying is that an early blowout
is better than a slow leak.

Dr. James Dobson,
Love Must Be Tough

Static silence filled the room as Denise felt the rage build inside her. Her body began to tremble as sixteen years of pent-up pain pushed against her will to hold it in. She glanced at Eric, then at her counselor with a silent plea for help, but Carol said nothing. Finally Denise could hold it no longer. She swiveled to face her husband.

"I've had it!" she shouted. "I've had it with your emotional unfaithfulness, and I've had it with your excuses! I did not cause your problem! You're an adult, and whether you like it or not, you alone are responsible! You're going to have to choose once and for all between me and the pornography. And if you choose the pornography, you're going to have to get out!"

Looking back on that day two years ago, Denise says:

> The words just kept tumbling out of my mouth, and I felt it way down inside. It was hard, because I had no job, we had two daughters, and my health wasn't good. It was incredibly frightening. But I felt empowered by finally confronting him. I was determined not to keep living that way, and that determination finally outweighed my fear of the unknown.
>
> Eric was furious. He told me he would not move out, that I was the one who would have to leave. But by the end of that counseling session, he said he was leaving us. Fortunately, God had other plans for our family.
>
> That day I had scheduled back-to-back appointments with two different therapists I'd been seeing. For some reason, Eric agreed to go to the second session with me. This wise counselor asked me to share my anger with Eric again, then she told me to go underneath my anger and express what was there. It was pure pain. I didn't want to divulge those feelings to Eric because I felt so vulnerable—so emotionally naked. I couldn't hold back my tears. She kept telling me to look at Eric and tell him what I was feeling, so I told him how hurt I was, how lonely I was, and how betrayed I felt. I told him how jealous I was of the other women, knowing that while the girls and I looked forward to him coming home after work, he stayed out with the women in his magazines, giving them his full attention. And I told him I wanted him to have eyes only for me.

What Is a Confrontation?

What Denise did that day is called a confrontation or intervention. Dr. Harry Schaumburg, author of *False Intimacy*, describes confrontation this way:

> It's a meeting between you and your spouse in which you (or your counselor) carry out a carefully planned sequence of steps designed to motivate your spouse to seek professional counseling. It's a time when you attempt to discuss the sexually addictive problems with your spouse, show support, and communicate in a firm but loving way that he or she must deal with the addiction through counseling.[1]

Because it broke through unplanned, Denise's confrontation wasn't the kind that's delivered in the calm, yet firm spirit recommended by the sexual addiction experts in this chapter, but it was a confrontation, nonetheless. And God honored it. Here's how Eric later described that day.

In the first session I responded in anger. I was furious that Denise was trying to tell me what to do. But by the second session, I think God had started to work in my heart and enabled me to hear her pain. It was as if for the first time I had ears to hear. That day, my denial was finally broken.

The counselor gave me a copy of a 12-Step recovery program that helps people who struggle with lust and sexual addiction. I vowed to start such a group in my area. I really didn't want to lose my family. I contacted another guy I knew who had the same problem, and we started to meet once a week.

That was two years ago, and during this time others have joined us. What the program and its literature has done is confront me for the first time with the fact that I have to take personal responsibility for my thoughts and actions. I stopped buying pornography, and I started crying out to God about how this addiction had me under its control.

Months later, I patted myself on the back for being sober from pornography, but I was still unwilling to give up compulsive masturbation. Coming to the place of willingness to let that go, too, to turn it over to God and step off into what felt to me like oblivion, was excruciating, but it has been worth it.

Why Confront?

There are many good reasons to meet the problem head-on with a well-planned confrontation. Because the cost is so high, the future of your marriage may literally be at stake.

"It's vital that your spouse receive professional counseling for intrusive and/or nonintrusive sexually addictive behaviors," writes Dr. Schaumburg. "Through a carefully planned intervention, you may be able to play a key role in helping your spouse . . . recognize the seriousness of the problem and choose to receive help."[2]

To Avoid Enabling the Sin

Dr. Mark Laaser, one of the leading Christian experts on sexual addiction and a man who has learned from his own broken experience, says, "If you suspect someone of being a sexual addict, you must get them help before they further destroy themselves and others." He then goes a step further and adds, "To ignore this behavior would be to become a party to their sin."[3]

Author and counselor David Augsburger tells how forgiving the offender too quickly can also make us an enabler of the sin. In writing about the cycle in addictions, he says, "In this cycle, forgiveness is the heart of the pathology. . . .

So forgiveness can be aiding, abetting, and enabling. Forgiveness is the central function of the enabler."[4]

Love Demands It

Dr. James Dobson believes that confrontation is the price of love. He says, "I must report the facts as I see them. *A passive approach often leads to the dissolution of the relationship.* Genuine love *demands* toughness in moments of crisis."[5]

Author Nancy Groom agrees: "When we genuinely love," she says, "we don't allow others to harm or abuse us— not just because we don't like it but also because it fails to invite the perpetrators to repentance and change. They may dislike the limits we set in love, but we can be genuinely unselfish in refusing to be victimized."[6]

To Motivate Change

I think Dr. Dobson gives the best reason to find the courage required to confront the addicted person. "It is only when he becomes miserable that he will accept the responsibility for change," Dobson says. "It is only when he sees everything of value to him—his home, his children, his wife, his reputation—begin to slip away that his choices will become clear. . . . What I am saying is that an early blowout is better than a slow leak!"[7]

God healed Pam and Richard Crist's marriage after years of sexual sin. Now counselors in the Seattle area, Rich and Pam shared their story on our *Love Under Fire* radio show. Rich told how God honored the way Pam confronted him.

> We had moved to Colorado and we both started hanging out in nightclubs and the drinking started again. And for me the pornography, sexual addiction, and chasing just really got out of hand again. Pam decided to go on a vacation, and she brought the three

children by herself up to the Seattle area to visit family. The second or third night of the trip, she tried to reach me at home—tried until about two in the morning—but I wasn't there.

The next day she contacted me at our business and she said, "Rich, I need to know where you were last night."

I don't know what came over me; I don't know if I wanted to get caught, or if I just didn't care, but I blurted out, "Well, I had an affair last night."

She said, "That's it. It's the out I've been looking for. Rich, I'm not coming home. This marriage is over." And I remember that there was a silence on the line, and I thought in that split moment of all the things that I thought I wanted out of life, all the things that I thought would bring me happiness—my children, my wife. And I realized I had just lost everything.

Today, Rich is deeply grateful for Pam's confrontation. It was the beginning of a whole new life, filled with love, healing, and ministry.

Consequences Will Only Get Worse

As hard as it is to hear, your husband's addiction won't just get better or go away without direct confrontation. It will only get worse, and your marriage will take a downhill slide, right along with his behavior. If you don't intervene and assist your husband in receiving help, you become an accomplice to his addiction. So many women's stories reflect this reality. Again and again I hear it. Rich shares how this was true in his life before Pam confronted him.

It became a private life to me. I don't know if you've ever heard about compartmentalizing our lives, but it was like I would walk through a door and

I would have this separate life that was going on, now with drugs and the alcohol, and I would walk back through it, and I would think to myself, "As long as I'm not bothering anyone else, this is a private life that doesn't hurt anyone else." During that time I continued as an active Christian in the other parts of my life. I even went downtown regularly and preached on street corners in Phoenix, Arizona.

Left unconfronted, this sort of double life can only get worse.

Confrontation Will Help You

Confrontation not only invites your husband to change, it will benefit you as well. Dr. Dobson understands this:

You will feel better because you will now be in control of the situation. There is no greater agony than journeying through a vale of tears, waiting in vain for the phone to ring or for a miracle to occur. Instead, the person has begun to respect [her]self and receive small evidences of respect in return. Even though it is difficult to let go once and for all, there are ample rewards for doing so. One of those advantages involves the feeling that [s]he has a plan—a program—a definite course of action to follow. That is infinitely more comfortable than experiencing the utter despair of powerlessness that [s]he felt before. And little by little, the healing process begins.[8]

What Does the Bible Say about Confrontation?

The Bible is our ultimate authority as we contemplate confrontation, and Matthew 18:15–17 (NIV) provides the wisdom and guidance we need:

If your brother sins against you, go and show him his fault, just between the two of you. If he listens to you, you have won your brother over. But if he will not listen, take one or two others along, so that "every matter may be established by the testimony of two or three witnesses." If he refuses to listen to them, tell it to the church; and if he refuses to listen even to the church, treat him as you would a pagan or a tax collector.

This passage makes it clear that we are not to look the other way, deny reality, or to wring our hands and wonder why God doesn't do something. Rather, it places the responsibility on us. We are told to confront the sin. Harry Schaumburg reminds us that the confrontation is ultimately motivated by love.

Always remember this: *The main reason for your intervention will be to encourage your spouse to obtain the help he or she needs.* As long as you have a relationship that can be salvaged, you will basically want to communicate to your spouse, "I'm committed to you, to seeing your life restored, to strengthening our relationship together, to getting closer to you and God in a stronger spiritual relationship."[9]

And author and counselor Dr. Willard Harley addresses some of our spiritual concerns when he writes:

Don't put up with the affair for another minute. . . . Often people who have strong religious convictions tell me "My church doesn't allow divorce." "God wants us to stay married. The Bible clearly teaches that divorce is a sin." . . . At the same time people must understand that once an affair has begun, the marriage has already been breached. What God has joined together, some man (or woman) has put asunder. If you want to put it back together, you have to take definite action. I urge wives in particular to take a hard, independent line and be willing to separate from their husbands temporarily until they can solve this matter together. Whatever they do, they must make it clear to the straying spouse that they will not put up with this.[10]

"But I'm Afraid"

Many women whose husbands are involved in sexual sin are afraid that if they confront his behavior, they will be left destitute and unable to cope with the ramifications in their lives. Often, risk does exist. If your husband is controlling, especially with money and family finances, confronting requires not only courage but planning and possibly even outside financial assistance. Others fear violent reactions, and this is another good reason to rely on a counselor to help stage the confrontation. Most are also afraid of what other people will think, especially the people at church. Not only does admitting your husband's sexual misconduct often result in embarrassment, humiliation, and shame for him, many women rightfully wonder how they will be treated by the church if their marriage troubles are revealed.

It's hard for us to see through the fog that shrouds the price of doing nothing. But we must ask, what will it cost you and others—emotionally, spiritually, relationally, and quite probably, physically—if the behavior continues? Who might your husband's activities harm in the future? Living with a husband's sexual sin extinguishes the light in your soul, little by little, day by day. You numb your pain. You steel yourself for the sake of the children. You may plead with your spouse and cry out to God, all the while hoping and praying things will get better.

After many years of working with married couples, Dr. Dobson describes some people's reactions this way:

> As love [in the marriage] begins to deteriorate, the vulnerable partner is inclined to panic. Characteristic responses include grieving, lashing out, begging, pleading, grabbing and

holding; or the reaction may be just the opposite, involving appeasement and passivity.[11]

Jennifer, a woman whose husband had multiple affairs, remembers how she panicked when she realized her husband was going to leave her.

> Over the days and weeks after he left I felt overwhelmed by what was happening. I had no one to support me emotionally. Swamped with pain, fear, and loneliness, I tried to retract my confrontation. I tried bargaining with him, pleading with him to try going to counseling with me for two months, then one month; finally I lowered it to two weeks. I was floundering. Finally I said, "Please come home. You can have your girlfriends."

"While these reactions are natural and understandable," says Dr. Dobson, "they are rarely successful in repairing the damage that has occurred. In fact, such reactions are usually counter-productive, destroying the relationship the threatened person is trying so desperately to preserve. . . . *Respect*, the critical ingredient in human affairs, is generated by quiet dignity, self-confidence, and common courtesy. It is assassinated by hand wringing, groveling in the dirt, and pleas for mercy."[12]

One pastor's wife named Dianna somehow found the strength needed for a quiet but firm confrontation. She described how the drama initially unfolded:

> My mom and I were grocery shopping at a store close to our church when the church secretary tracked me down in one of the aisles and said "I need you to come with me. Your mom should take care of your car and the kids for a while." I asked, "What's going on?" and she answered, "I can't tell you." "Well,

just tell me if it's Steve or somebody else," I asked, and she answered, "It's Steve."

So Mom took the kids, and I got in the car with the secretary, and I just knew down deep what was going on. I said, "Is Steve having an affair?" But she said, "I can't say, Dianna." We got to the house and got out of the car—it's amazing what you can do when you're in shock—I think it had already set in for me, so we walked into the house and Steve was standing there with this other man. I said, "What's going on?" And Steve said, "I've been having an affair."

I wasn't surprised. Shocked, but not surprised, if you know what I mean. At first I was tempted to leave, and then as I asked more questions, I thought, "You know, I'm not the one who did this, and I'm going to stay here with the kids, and I would like Steve to leave." So I told him he needed to leave and he packed up and moved out.

That quiet confrontation began a long journey toward health and healing. God saved this family and today they have rebuilt their marriage, they're back in ministry, and are helping other couples in crises.

The Need for a Counselor

With a compassionate heart, Dr. Schaumburg cautions, "When you take action, you may feel as if you are tearing your life apart, and you will need the support of a counselor. You may feel almost like a prosecutor in a courtroom, even though your goal is to help your spouse overcome his . . . addiction. Your world will be shaken up and turned upside down."[13]

It's normal to feel fear just thinking about a confrontation or intervention. And for many reasons, you shouldn't even attempt to do one alone. You need support and assistance if you are to succeed. This chapter is presented only as a summary of a confrontational approach that a wife may take in dealing with her husband's habitual inappropriate sexual behaviors or sexual addiction. It is not comprehensive or exhaustive. It is highly recommended that you consider consultation with a professional therapist and possibly an attorney who is experienced in this area before you confront a spouse with this problem. If at all possible, find a Christian counselor who is trained to deal with sexually addictive behaviors. Such a person may be hard to find in your area, so ask for referrals from others who may be able to help you.

Unfortunately, professional counseling is usually expensive. If you have health insurance, check your plan to see what may be covered. Plans vary greatly, so it's important to fully understand your own. If you don't have insurance, or if the counseling is just too expensive for you, call your local crisis line, or its equivalent, in your area. I volunteer at our Seattle crisis line, and I know that similar help lines stretch across the United States, and in many other countries as well. Such services usually have a database identifying which counselors will provide services on a sliding fee scale, or for a low flat rate.

An excellent Christian resource is The Christian Alliance for Sexual Recovery in Tupelo, Mississippi. They offer a variety of helps for families dealing with sexual issues. See appendix 3 at the end of this book for more information.

For more information, or possibly even help, call the Sex Addicts Anonymous or Sex and Love Addicts Anonymous number in your area. You'll probably need to call the national number (it's listed in appendix 3) or your crisis line to get it, and you'll probably have to leave a message when you do call. Be sure to state that they are *only* to talk to you when they call back. Anyone involved in either of these organizations guards confidentiality above all else, and they will protect your request.

Also, larger churches sometimes have professional counselors on staff who might work with you. Your pastor might also be a willing resource. Not every pastor understands the nature of addictions, but if yours does, he might be able to help you with the confrontation. Amy's pastor was ready, willing, and able, for which she's deeply grateful. On our broadcast, she explained how her pastor helped her confront her husband:

> My husband and I had been married for about twelve years when I discovered he was addicted to pornography. I came home from work one day and opened the mail and surprise, surprise, there was a package containing a pornographic videotape. I'm very methodical so I called the company that had sent the tape to make sure it wasn't a mistake, and they said it wasn't. My husband is a Christian, and that night he was at an elders' meeting at the church. So I called the church and told the pastor that he needed to come home with my husband, and told him what I'd found. And so our pastor did, and we confronted my husband. At first he did the standard denial thing, then anger, and finally brokenness.

It's been two years since Amy's discovery and confrontation, and today her family is happy and whole. Amy's no-nonsense attitude and her willingness to reach out for help provides a model for all of us because it's *very* difficult to confront alone. Mark Laaser makes that clear when he writes:

Dr. Richard Irons of Golden Valley Health Center says that individually confronting addicts is like playing one-on-one basketball against Michael Jordan. We won't win. They are too skilled at denial and delusion. He said, however, that when we take a team of people, even if none of them are NBA caliber, the team will probably get the job done. . . . The elements of two or more people confronting the sexual addict are identical to the individual intervention. Every person in the room would simply take turns stating care and concern, providing evidence, defining boundaries, laying down consequences, and offering help.[14]

A Wife's Sample Confrontation

Before any confrontation, Dr. Dobson cautions that a wife must change the way she approaches her husband so that he sees a woman with firm boundaries and strong self-respect. Dobson says, "The precipitated crisis, first, must be accompanied by an entire change of attitude. Instead of begging, pleading, wringing of your hands and whimpering like an abused puppy, you as the vulnerable partner must appear strangely calm and assured."[15]

Some experts also recommend that you put in writing the words you plan to say to your husband ahead of time. Not only will this help you stay focused when you confront him, a letter becomes a permanent document for him to reread as he considers the cost of his sexual acting out.

The following sample confrontation provides a synthesis of those contained in several of the resources cited in this chapter. You may use these words directly or adapt them for your personal situation.

"What you have done (describe the exact nature of the wrong) has hurt me deeply, and I am very angry. Nonetheless, I need for you to be honest with me and tell me the full extent of your sexual behaviors."

"I'm not judging you and I don't want to hear your defense, I just want you to hear what I'm saying and feeling. I want you to know what this has done to me."

"As my husband, I expect you to be sexually and emotionally faithful to me, both in thought and action."

"If you continue what I believe are sexually inappropriate behaviors, you will have to move out."

"I love you and I value the life we have together, but in order for you to continue living here, you must stop your activity and you must get professional help immediately. Here is a list of professionals who can help you." (Include counselors, treatment centers, and 12-Step groups such as those sponsored by the American Family Association and Sex Addicts Anonymous. See resources in appendix 3.)

"I do love you, and I want our marriage to make it. I hope and pray that you will choose to get help so that our life together can continue."

Some wives won't want their marriages to continue, even if their husbands get help. These feelings can be especially strong early in the recovery process. But often, even the woman who thinks she can't possibly stay in the relationship finds hope and healing as she sees her husband and her marriage begin to change. Amy, whose husband had ordered the pornographic video, describes her feelings immediately following the confrontation:

> At that point, I wasn't sure my marriage was going to make it, or if I even wanted it to. I went to workshops, got a lot of help, came home, still was not sure about the marriage. But I can say now, almost two years into recovery, that I'm actually thankful for what I went through. If God had said, "Amy, do you want to choose this?" I would have certainly said "No." But now I have a closer relationship with my heavenly Father, and I have a much closer relationship with my husband than I ever did all those earlier years.

Now What?

Again, Dr. Dobson gently encourages us. He says:

> By making it clear that there are limits to what you can tolerate, you are showing self-respect and confidence. The key word is *confidence,* and it is of maximum importance. Your manner should say, "I believe in me. I'm no longer afraid. I can cope, regardless of the outcome. I know something I'm not talking about. I've had my day of sorrow and I'm through crying. God and I can handle whatever life puts in the path."[16]

Dr. Dobson describes the "you" your husband needs to see. He needs to believe you mean what you say, and so do you. While this kind of courageous behavior will have the added benefit of making you feel stronger, it won't dry all your tears. The pain you're feeling can't be wiped away that easily. Grieving is a process and takes time. We'll look at that process in depth in chapter 8, and at how your support group can play a key role in helping you through it.

During the days, weeks, and months following the confrontation, remind yourself that change is a process; it's going to take time and hard work for your husband to rebuild his life and his relationship with God. Recognize that everything can't be solved at once. Many factors led to his inappropriate sexual behaviors, and his healing will require the help of a man, or a group of men, to walk with him and hold him accountable as he develops new spiritual muscles. He will probably also need a Christian counselor, and hopefully, your pastor will support him as well. It will take time and commitment for you and your husband to work through the past and renew your marriage and family life. Remember, confrontation is just the first step.

The painful truth remains that no matter how carefully and prayerfully a woman follows the guidance of Scripture and the Christian experts, her husband may choose not to change; he may choose to turn and walk away from her and their family. All we can do is follow the steps as directed in Matthew 18:15–17, acknowledge our inability to control our husbands, and put our trust in God, knowing he will never leave us nor forsake us—and that no matter what the future holds, he'll be there to lean on and give comfort.

--5--

Rebuilding
Your Self-Esteem

You, Me, and the Lingerie Models

Faith is . . . Remembering I am God's priceless
treasure when I feel utterly worthless.

Pamela Reeve

As I pulled into the church parking lot,
I wondered what Toni would be like.
*So many hurting women, each with a
slightly different story,* I thought. I spotted the white mini-
van she said she'd be driving and pulled into the empty space
beside it. She looked up and smiled when I caught her eye.

Toni got out of her car and waited uncertainly as I
approached. *Hmm,* I thought, *attractive, early thirties maybe.
Well, whatever her husband did to hurt her, he didn't do it
because of the way she looks.* We greeted each other and chat-
ted as she took me to the counseling room the church secretary said we could use for our meeting.

As we settled into the overstuffed chairs that were placed
opposite each other, I leaned forward and said, "Well, Toni,
what's going on?" And she began to spill out her story.

My husband, Roger, is a youth pastor. One of the most hurtful experiences I've had in the five years we've been married happened two weeks ago, and I can't seem to shake off the hurt and anger I feel. I heard you and your husband on the radio and I thought maybe you could help me.

It happened at a college-age retreat we were leading for our church. I thought we were going there as a unit—two people who loved each other and wanted to minister to a group of young people. When we met a beautiful young woman with this gorgeous honey-colored hair cascading over her shoulders, I thought, *Wow, I'll bet she drives the guys crazy this week!*

At first I didn't think too much about the way she kept finding reasons to sit next to Roger at meals and to ask him questions during the breaks. Roger and I have, or I thought we had, a rule we follow—neither of us counsels the opposite sex. So I felt confident that try as she may, this young woman wasn't going to corner my husband alone.

But by dinnertime on Tuesday, I was getting pretty irritated at her behavior and I let Roger know it. Then Wednesday night when the evening finally ended around 11:00 P.M., I told Roger I was going to go ahead to our cabin and start getting ready for bed. He said, "Okay, honey, I'll be there in a few minutes."

At 12:15 he still wasn't back to our cabin; I was tired but didn't want to go to bed until we'd had a chance to talk about the day. So I decided to look for him. I put my coat on over my nightgown and went to find out when he'd be coming. There was a light on in the chapel so I headed there first. When I opened the door I could hardly believe my eyes—that gorgeous young woman was crying in Roger's arms! I was crushed. In that moment, my self-esteem plummeted. It's like something inside me curled up and died. All the trust I'd

placed in him to love and cherish me disappeared in an
instant, and I felt like my self-esteem went with it. The
scene that followed was really ugly and we still haven't
been able to deal with it.

Toni's plummeting self-esteem after observing her husband's behavior is not much different than most other
women's in a similar situation. Betrayal hurts, whether it's
emotional or sexual. It's not unusual to doubt your attrac-
tiveness, desirability, or worthiness when you find out your
husband is tempted by other women, or has actually given
in to that temptation. Some men even cruelly compare their
wives to other women. One woman told me her husband
compared her to the woman he was having an affair with:
The wife is a size fourteen and the other woman, who is
ten years younger, is a size one. His comparison shredded
the little self-esteem she had left.

Sexual Sin's Impact on Self-Esteem

When we marry, we want and need to believe that our
husbands will always feel and act like we are the only woman
he'll ever have eyes for, and it hurts when we discover that
isn't always true. In *Surviving Infidelity*, Gloria Harris and
Rona Subotnik describe the impact an affair has on a woman's self-esteem:

> We place our trust in our partners and believe they will not
> betray us. So when infidelity occurs, it is a breach of sacred
> vows, and we are aware that trust in the marriage has died. . . .
> When this happens, it is only human to question your self-
> worth. The betrayed partner may feel rejected and humili-
> ated. . . . unloved, and powerless. You may begin to doubt your
> attractiveness, desirability, or worthiness.[1]

One young wife who had recently discovered her husband's
years-long affair with her best friend summed up what many

women feel. With pain leaking out between her words, she said simply, "I'm not feeling very attractive these days."

Discovering that your husband is involved in *any kind* of extramarital sexual activity—even mental activity—can shatter your self-esteem, leaving only a fragmented view of your worth. When we're wounded this deeply, we may believe that we're fundamentally flawed. "After all, didn't the man who knows me best need something or someone else to be satisfied?" we ask. And often we seek the answer by checking out the competition—a habit that can crucify our self-worth. Robin has developed this debilitating habit.

> Ever since I found out about Corky's sexual fantasizing, I examine other women. It doesn't matter where I am, the first thing I do is scope out the "competition." What are they wearing? How beautiful are they? How do I compare? Would my Corky be more attracted to them than he is to me? And if he's with me and a beautiful woman is present, I panic. All I can think about is what's going through his mind. Is he going to be thinking of her the next time we make love?

Alan Loy McGinnis captures the shattering impact of the comparison game in his book, *Confidence.*

> There is probably no other habit that chips away at our self-confidence so effectively as the habit of scanning the people around us to see how we compare. It is as if we have a radar dish on our foreheads, constantly searching to see if someone else is quicker, tanner, or brighter. And when we find that at times someone is, we are devastated. And our self-esteem sinks lower.[2]

Childhood Issues Return

When a husband is involved in sexually inappropriate activities, the pain taps into our life history, connecting with negative messages and hurtful experiences from the past. And it can take a lot of hard work to move beyond the connection of those memories and messages, as it did for Beth.

> My husband's sexual addiction has forced me to deal with the painful parts of my childhood. Both my father and mother abused me—each in a different way. Sexual abuse left me with poor self-esteem and tremendous anger—anger that spilled out on other people. It took counseling and group work to deal with those feelings: the hurt, the anger, and the damaged self-esteem. I had to grieve those childhood losses before I could move toward the healing needed because of Wendell's addiction. His affairs, pornography use, visiting prostitutes, and other activities felt like proof that I wasn't valuable. I used to feel guilty because I was taking up space in the world, and I still work hard to feel good about myself. I think I probably will for the rest of my life, but God has done a wonderful work in my heart, and because of it, I've been able to forgive my husband.

We're especially vulnerable to developing damaged self-esteem in childhood, as Alan McGinnis observes: "Regardless of how well parents do by their children, it seems that most people reach young adulthood feeling, 'You're OK but I'm not OK.' It is almost part of the human equipment."[3] And for those whose parents do more harm than good, outside help is needed.

We each hold a scrap bag full of memory swatches, woven from childhood pain and negative messages. And now our husbands' words and actions become entwined with our history, tightening the weave of the seeming truth, and our minds go to work like antique sewing machines. Pumping mental needles up and down, they stitch musty memories onto the tear-stained fabric of our present pain. Now draped in our creations, we feel isolated, unattractive, and different.

Society's Messages

When we discover our husbands struggle with sexual issues, we are suddenly aware that everywhere they look, temptation awaits them—in magazines and movies, on television and the Internet, at the beach, at work, and on the street. In this society, there's no way to escape it; we're surrounded by sensuality. This, too, can affect our self-esteem.

We live in a land that places a huge emphasis on looks and sexiness, as defined by being young, slender, and beautiful. Yet I read recently that the odds of being born a homecoming queen, Hollywood beauty, or supermodel are, at best, one in ten thousand. That means that for every woman with all the elements that society exalts, 9,999 of us fall short. We simply can't compete with the physical perfection placed before our husbands.

Not long ago, I videotaped several TV commercials to make a similar point in a women's seminar I presented on the East Coast. I was amazed at how easily I found the footage of what I needed. I taped one commercial for Victoria's Secret lingerie in which young, lean, female bodies danced seductively in nylon briefer than your underwear. I couldn't resist calling my husband into the room.

"Honey, you've got to come and see this," I called. "I can't believe it's on television!" After watching for a few moments, Pat turned and walked away, saying, "I'm glad *you* can use that clip. There's no way I could show it at any of my men's seminars without making every man in the room stumble!"

Is it any wonder that when our husbands are tempted, we begin to search our bathroom mirrors for reflections of ourselves that prove we are good enough? Every wife wants to be physically attractive to her husband, but we want to be loved for our *whole* selves as well. Author Colette Dowling said it well for all of us: "We still long to be seen as [women] separate and individual, to be loved for our uniqueness—and ordinariness. To be accepted with our anxieties, our inevitable setbacks, our flaws."[4]

But does our need to feel good about ourselves—to have positive self-esteem—run counter to the biblical perspective? I don't believe it does.

Scriptural Basis for Self-Esteem

Our heavenly Father conveyed how precious and valuable each of us is when he sent his son to the cross on our behalf. Throughout Scripture, he calls us "the apple of his eye" and "his beloved." Psalm 139:14 tells us we were "fearfully and wonderfully made" (NIV). If the God of creation believes we're worth dying for, shouldn't we recognize and claim that worth? How can we doubt his words and actions on our behalf?

"Do you realize that you are one of a kind?" ask the authors of *The Child in Each of Us.*

> There has never been nor will there ever be someone exactly like you, with the same sum total of your feelings, attitudes, experiences, character traits, hopes, dreams, and goals. Think of it. No carbon copy. No mass-produced duplicate. Just one and only *you.* . . . When God created us in his own image, he purposely designed us with distinct personalities. No poor imitations or cookie-cutter creations for him. No reprints, replicas, or reproductions. Each person would be an original, one of a kind, with the inherent worth of an original work of art crafted by the master Craftsman.[5]

That means that no matter what our husbands do, no matter how we compare to a perfect beauty, we're the precious and valuable work of our Creator.

The Value of Positive Self-Esteem

Positive self-esteem plays a crucial role in our lives. It helps us cope with life's disappointments, it generates emotional energy to relate to others, to do our work, and to enjoy life. It's required to do nearly everything, and in the wake of a husband's sexual sin, we need it even more.

After hearing about an Arizona woman named Maggie who has a wonderful recovery story, I called and asked if we could talk. She was warm and friendly and told me about her marriage and her life since then. After sixteen years of living with her abusive, sexually unfaithful husband, she had no idea of who she was or what she wanted to do; she was completely without goals, energy, or zest for life.

> Early in my therapy, my counselor asked, "What does Maggie like to do?" I couldn't answer her—I didn't know! "Whatever," was all I could say. I could tell you what was wrong with me, I just couldn't tell you what was right. Brad blamed me for his affairs, and I blamed myself. He told me I wasn't thin enough, wasn't pretty enough, that I was boring and that the women at work were more exciting. My self-esteem was in the toilet. He even said, "You'd have to pay somebody to sleep with you." My self-esteem plummeted even lower. I felt that there was no one out there who would ever want me.
>
> Slowly, my counselor helped me learn to value and take care of myself. She put grains of truth out there and let them hang until I was ready to look at them. To help me see that I did many things right, she had me put a piece of paper on my bathroom mirror and write down things as I accomplished them. I had discounted everything I did, but the lists made me realize I did do meaningful, productive things during each day.

Our wounded self-esteem can find healing, but healing requires a response not just to the way we look but to our whole selves. Loving, accepting, supportive relationships play a vital role in providing that response, and in helping us challenge the messages—from the past, the present, and within.

Support Groups and Self-Esteem

Self-identity germinates in relationships. Healthy, affirming relationships—those in which people give each other the right to their feelings and the sense that they have value—those relationships nurture healthy self-esteem. But the relationships in a good support group go a step further; they provide a relational greenhouse where parched and wilted self-esteem can be gently nurtured back to life. Health care professionals recognize that healing flourishes under the light and warmth of loving support.

A Place to Heal

Dr. Bessel van der Kok, director of the Massachusetts Mental Health Trauma Center, said, "If victims have a receptive social support network which does not blame them for their misfortunes and can help them to mourn the loss of loved ones, or feelings of relative impotence, they are likely to recover from the trauma . . . if both internal strengths and external supports are optimally available, some sort of resolution is usually achieved."[6]

Loving support helped Sandy Wilson's self-esteem survive when her Christian psychologist husband's affair came to light. She writes about her experience in *Restoring the Fallen*.

> It was clear to me that we could not walk down this path alone.
> . . . I also needed some close friends to come around me on a
> daily basis. I needed someone to listen, to validate my pain,

to pray for me, to tell me Earl's choices were not my fault, to let me vent my anger and frustration, to help me make practical decisions. The three women friends I invited to enter my shattered world fleshed out Jesus' love to me consistently and faithfully over the next several years. Each in her own unique way was there for me.

I remember one occasion when I felt overwhelmed by discouragement. One of those friends just held me for a long time. She gave me no answers, she made no promises, she just helped me feel love and comfort. Somehow her love instilled hope in me and broke through my despair.

These friends (and several couples in whom we confided and who stuck by us) became even more important after Earl's sin became public and I was abandoned by a number of other friends and colleagues. Some people rallied to support Earl, who was open about his brokenness and devastation, but they seemed clueless about my needs and even avoided me. Some blamed me for Earl's choices. Still others vented their anger toward Earl by telling me how they felt but refusing to confront Earl. This created even more anger and confusion within me. But the rejection and insensitivity I experienced at times was offset by the loving kindness of my faithful friends. They were also invaluable in reaffirming my worth as a person and rebuilding my shattered self-esteem. The role of friends like these in the aftermath of such brokenness cannot be underestimated.[7]

When we interviewed Sandy and her husband on our radio show, Sandy and I talked about the impact a husband's behavior can have on a wife. I said to Sandy, "As we get older, it's especially hard to maintain our self-esteem, isn't it?"

"I wouldn't know!" She laughed and then said, "I couldn't resist that!" It was obvious from the joy and freedom in her voice on the air that day that God had wonderfully healed her wounded self-esteem.

A Place to Be Told It's Not Our Fault

It's ironic, but like Sandy, many women receive a portion of the blame for their husband's moral failure. This was Maggie's experience.

> Most of the people in my life were less than supportive. The people at Brad's office didn't say it out loud, but their faces reflected pity, as if they were thinking, "Oh, poor Maggie." I didn't even tell my parents for two months because I was afraid of what they'd say. And when I did, my mother was furious at me for letting Brad treat me the way he had; she said to me, "I've lost all respect for you." My dad had mixed feelings but felt I had somehow let Brad down. His response was, "Men will be men. You're supposed to overlook things like that." And my sister, who is nine years younger, revealed that Brad had tried to sleep with her before she was married. She hadn't wanted to hurt me by telling me before.

When we meet with a lack of care and understanding, a personal support system—like Sandy's—becomes crucial if we hope to survive with our self-esteem intact.

A Place to Learn to Be Assertive

Maggie's wonderful counselor also helped her learn these tough lessons. She shared these insights about her healing process.

> My counselor taught me about boundaries and how to draw them. By this time, Brad had moved across the country with his girlfriend, but sometimes he would call me about some business he needed to accomplish here. He'd say, "I need for you to do this

and this and this for me," and I would do it. My counselor would ask, "Why are you doing this?"

"Because he asked me to," was all I could reply. I
didn't see that I had choices, and it was up to me to
make them. And when he came back into town from
time to time I would have his favorite beverage in the
refrigerator for him. He'd come here and try to get
me to go to bed with him, then get mad at me when
I said no.

To teach me how to stand up to him, my therapist
role-played with me. She pretended to be Brad and
I had to say no to her demands. My voice shook—I
was terrified just pretending she was Brad! We had
to do it over and over, but eventually I grew stronger.

It's important to understand the difference between
healthy self-love and narcissism, and between assertiveness
and aggressiveness. Jesus told us to love others as we love
ourselves. Healthy self-love involves respecting and valu-
ing God's creative workmanship within us. Assertiveness
is merely the quiet, confident defense of our right to be
treated with respect as a child of God who is precious to
her heavenly Father.

Authors Harris and Subotnik explain that, "People feel
much better about themselves when they become more
assertive. Assertiveness is the middle ground between two
extremes: nonassertiveness and aggressiveness. It communicates two-way respect—respect for yourself and respect for
others . . . As assertiveness increases . . . so does self-esteem."[8]

A Place to Deal with Negative Memories and Messages

Healing old memories and silencing old voices takes
commitment and hard work, work that is almost impossible to do alone. But when we drag memories and messages
into the light with others who support us, those old mes-

sages lose their power, freeing us to utilize one another's unconditional love to reprogram them. In chapter 8 we look more closely at how to heal emotional wounds. Healing sometimes requires professional help, but often a loving support group can begin to provide the safety and encouragement that's needed.

As we do this tough work, we finally reach a place where we know that we're loved for who we are, and our self-esteem grows stronger. Then, with a healthier self-image, we find the freedom we need to make the choices that lead to change.

A Place to Examine Our Options

When our husbands' actions have hurt us, it's easy to see ourselves as victims without choices. Sticking to that victim role can glue us to our pain. But if we can move beyond blaming and take responsibility for new choices, support people can help us recognize what options exist. And when we become aware of available choices, new possibilities open to us, and our group's prayer and encouragement gives us the courage to initiate change.

With her counselor's help, Maggie slowly let go of her victim role and a whole new life filled with opportunities and choices opened before her. This is the rest of her story.

> One day about six months after Brad left, I was in the kitchen singing and dancing, when one of my sons walked in. "Mom, are you stoned?" he asked. I realized he had never seen me happy before, and it spoke volumes about what his young life had been like. It took five years working with my counselor before I knew I could do it on my own, although I still go in occasionally for "tune-ups." As I grew, I knew I wanted to be able to help others, so I went back to school and became a counselor.

I want to encourage other hurting women to find a good counselor and begin going regularly. And to find a good support group because you need a place where you are accepted for who you are, and where love and affirmation counterbalance the hurt and pain. It humbles me knowing God can use me, and that he's bringing people to me who need help. I am reminded that in all things he really does work for good.

A Place to Reprogram Our Thoughts

Proverbs 23:7 tells us, "For as [a man or woman] thinketh in his heart, so is he" (KJV). But it wasn't until the twentieth century that science recognized this truth. We now understand that much of our behavior stems from our thoughts and beliefs.

Author Alan Loy McGinnis believes

What you hold in your mind is what you move toward. . . . It is variously called "mental rehearsal," "imagination," "visualization," and "visioning," and it is anything but a new discovery. The idea is as old as the Bible. . . . Some Christian writers recently have attacked this mental imaging as being somehow occult and non-Christian, but nothing could be further from the truth. The Scriptures admonish us again and again to pray with faith, and explain that the answer to our prayers will be in proportion to our belief. This way of "seeing" the event occur is one very concrete way of exercising that faith.[9]

This was beautifully modeled for me several years ago when my pastor had an affair with the church secretary, and ultimately left his wife, family, and the ministry to marry her. His wife, whom I'll call Nan, was a wonderful, effervescent Christian woman. In the weeks preceding her husband's final decision, she sat at the piano, playing for our praise and worship services, while tears streamed down her face as her heart and life broke apart. Yet most of the time, she wore her radiant smile. I remember asking her how she could smile when she was in so much pain, and I'll never forget her answer: "I've found that if I wear a smile, it may not change my circumstances, but it makes *me* feel better inside."

Nan was living out that Scripture "as [a man or woman] thinketh in his heart, so is he." No, her smile didn't change her circumstances, but it reflected her faith and hope in her heavenly Father who carried her through her life's most difficult experience.

Oh, to have Nan's faith. This doesn't mean that if we believe we don't hurt, we won't. We will experience a wide range of emotions as we grieve what our husbands' actions have taken from us. But by asking God to be our strength as we face our pain and then believing that he will be, he will lovingly move us toward healing and growth.

A Place to Develop and Grow

We have all been given inherent, God-given talents and natural abilities. Refining and using these abilities can provide a fountain of self-esteem because by using the gifts he gave us, we know we are honoring our Creator. Pastor Ron Lee Davis expressed this clearly when he wrote:

> God wants to encourage you to discover his healing for your broken self-image. As John Claypool has said, "To accept yourself positively and live creatively is the way to joy, but to deny and reject God's gift of yourself is the way to ruin." So when you arise each new morning, say a prayer of thanks to God for the gift of who you are. Focus on the joy of knowing God, of being a child of your loving Father. As God progressively discloses deeper and richer insights into your gifts and qualities as a special human being, you'll find . . . you really like the special person you are.[10]

A Place to Embrace God's Love and Acceptance

Our support group, above all else, is a place to embrace God's love and acceptance. He uses us in each other's lives to do this work. Not only will we find love and acceptance for ourselves, but we can also give it to one another. And with love and acceptance at work in our lives, God's healing will continue in us. This healing prepares us for the next step in our growth, the challenging step of self-examination, that crucial time when we turn the spotlight upon ourselves.

Changing the Only Person You Can Change

Sweeping Your Side of the Street

> You aren't responsible for anything that
> happened to you as a child.
> You are responsible for everything
> you do as an adult.
>
> *Susan Forward*

I first met Nancy on the waterfront in downtown Seattle. It was one of those glorious summer days we treasure here in the Pacific Northwest, because we have to endure so many gray ones. Over the phone, we had agreed to meet at a particular waterfront restaurant, each of us describing ourselves to the other. When I arrived, I spotted her sitting at an outside table on the pier, waiting for me while pigeons poked along near her feet, and noisy seagulls flew overhead, occasionally diving to scavenge a diner's dropped morsel.

"Hi, you must be Nancy. Isn't this a fabulous day?" I said, joining her under the table's red and white striped umbrella.

For a few moments, we gazed out at Puget Sound, blue and gold in the brilliant light, and watched ferries and sailboats plow languidly on the glazed surface. Then, for the next two hours, in the midst of the lunching locals and camera-laden vacationers, she told me her story.

Over the last three decades, Nancy had endured one of the worst marriages I've ever heard about. Now a year into her husband's recovery journey, she was still having trouble letting go of her pain and anger. Nonetheless, she was continuing to work. She willingly shared her story with me, hoping that it might be of help to other women. Of special importance was a difficult exchange she had had with her counselor several weeks ago. She begins her story with his words to her:

> My counselor said to me, "Nancy, I hear the hurt, and the pain, and the anger you feel because of Morgan's affairs, but you still need to take off your blinders and look at where you have failed, too. Until you do that, your failures will short-circuit your relationship with God."
>
> This wasn't the first time my counselor, Paul, had made this speech. And it still made me furious. I wanted to shout at him, "How dare you, after all I've been through with my husband! How dare you tell me to examine myself while he sleeps around all over town!"
>
> But slowly, over time I became convicted, especially about the way I talked to Morgan. I had really quit loving him a long time ago, after so many years filled with affairs, prostitutes, and pornography. Even though he hadn't done any of these things during the last year and he was committed to not falling back into sin, I still felt disgusted by him. There were times when I treated him awful; I said horrible things and often put

> him down. I guess it was my way of trying to get back at him. It took time before I recognized that in God's eyes sin is sin, which meant my attitude, too. When I began to tell Morgan how sorry I was for the way I treated him, God started changing our relationship. My anger didn't evaporate over night. Thirty years of heartache had me stuck. I tried and tried to let go of it, but I couldn't do it on my own. Finally, I begged God to take it away, telling him I couldn't do it. Miraculously, he did, without my even being aware of it. One day I just realized it was gone, and it felt so good to be free.

When we turn the spotlight on ourselves, we are choosing to stop our futile attempts to control our husbands and instead step under that bright light and take an honest look at ourselves. "Why," you may ask, "should I examine myself at a time like this? He's the one destroying our lives! I haven't done anything wrong!"

We look inward not to beat ourselves up or to endorse what he's done. We do it because it's only when we see our faults as our own, instead of in reaction to him, that we gain a clearer picture of who we are and what negative behaviors we've brought into the relationship. And once we focus on those behaviors, the denial is peeled from our eyes and we are freed to envision and embrace change. This change strengthens our relationship with God, removing things from our lives that block contact with him. And now, more than ever, we need all of God we can get.

How the Past Sets Up the Present

In the last chapter we looked at how painful childhood memories and messages can affect our self-esteem. They also impact us in another way. Therapist Michael Moore explains.

All of us are wounded sooner or later by life's afflictions. When we are wounded at an early age, we choose means of defense and coping which may have seemed the wisest of the choices we had in our grasp, but later proved to be our undoing. When adult responsibility and freedom should be available to us, instead we experience self-defeating, relationship-defeating, and choice-limiting patterns that compulsively resist our commonsense attempts at change. It is at this time that our defenses though *innocent when we learned them, are no longer innocent!* They harm our relationship to ourselves, others, and God.[1]

Cynthia Rowland McClure knows this well. A former TV journalist and author of *The Monster Within* and *The Courage to Go On,* she nearly lost her twelve-year battle with bulimia. Then a friend recommended she go to a Minirth-Meier clinic in Dallas, Texas. Three months later, Cynthia emerged free from her addiction, but also aware that Satan had used her childhood experiences to snare her with his bulimic monster. Grateful to God, she refocused her life's energy to share her story of hope through speaking and writing. As part of that powerful story, Cynthia tells people, "One important element I've learned is that I am what I am today because of the past. Whether it was good or bad, the past affects me today. And that's why it's vital for us to deal with the ghosts of the past."[2]

Coping Mechanisms

There's no way around it—as we grow up on this globe, we *all* experience emotional pain. And just as certainly, we react to it in some way. With only the limited understanding of a child, our responses—at best—are coping mechanisms. They are the best we can do as children, but they hang around and become a part of us. From them we form our relationship styles and the ways we deal with emotional pain.

For the fortunate among us, this cause-effect pattern plays itself out in ways that interfere but don't cripple us emotionally, relationally, or spiritually. But for others, deep emotional damage in childhood sets up addictions and choices that destroy lives and relationships. Nashville therapist Marnie Ferree shared her poignant story several months ago on our radio broadcast.

When I was three years old my mother died of cancer. My father, who was a minister, didn't know how to grieve so he just didn't, and he wouldn't let me and my two older brothers grieve, either. We never spoke of Mom as ever having been alive and a part of our family, and we never spoke of her death. If I said, "I miss Mommy," Dad would say, "Why? She's in a better place now." After her death, Dad poured himself into church work, I suppose as a way to deal with his own grief. We had enough money, but it was as if we had no parents.

Two years later, when I was five, a twenty-year-old young man came into our lives and became a dear family friend. He was deeply involved in our family's life for the next fifteen years and even lived with us for periods of time. For me, he became the father I never had. He had time for me—lots of it. He played with me, taught me to write, and encouraged my writing, which I eventually used by becoming a journalist. But he also abused me sexually. From the time I was five until I was twenty, he had a sexual relationship with me. I guess because it started so early, I never considered myself sexually abused. I loved this man; he was a part of our family. And when he married it broke my heart. I became very promiscuous. I was so needy and desperate for love, and I had learned from my friend that sex equals love.

When I was a freshman in college, I met Bob. He had a deep Christian faith and we both thought that

love and our Christianity would make our relationship
work, and we got married. It wasn't long until I found
out that Bob couldn't fill the hole in my heart.

On our first wedding anniversary I slept with his
best friend and continued that relationship for a while.
We eventually divorced, and a year later I married
David. We had two children and I chose to stay home
with them because David made plenty of money. I
was busy writing and speaking and we were active in
church. We were relatively happy for five years.

Marnie's story doesn't end there. Over the next several
years she had a series of affairs. Marnie finally got the help
she needed after two ominous experiences shook her to the
core: She was diagnosed with cervical cancer caused by a
sexually transmitted disease, and soon thereafter she read
a newspaper obituary for one of her past sexual partners
who had just died of AIDS. Despite those scares, changing wasn't easy. Marnie's childhood emptiness had been
soothed by sexual relationships, which then became the
coping mechanism she used to treat her emotional pain.
These learned habits ultimately affected the way she conducted all her male-female relationships.

We all have ways we treat our fear and pain. Maybe yours
is perfectionism, controlling others, worrying about what
people think, or flirting with men, but they are all wrong
and we need to take responsibility for them and begin the
change process. As Mark Luciano writes, "These defects
are not an indelible part of you or your character. . . . Aware-
ness of these unhealthy traits and the experiences from
which they arise is the beginning of a process of growing
out of them."[3]

By recognizing and understanding the origin of these
coping mechanisms, we pick up a powerful tool to use in
their deconstruction. We still must keep in mind, however,

that the behaviors *are* sin and we will need God's help to eliminate them.

Facing Our Own Shortcomings

Facing ourselves with all our flaws takes courage because our sin nature tries to justify our thoughts and actions. But face them we must, because as 1 John 1:8 warns, "If we claim to be without sin, we deceive ourselves and the truth is not in us" (NIV).

As a Christian since childhood, I thought I was aware of my weaknesses and failures and was giving them to God. But I couldn't see the parts of me that were still hiding behind my denial. (Or the parts of me that are *still* hiding there!) As I used all my spiritual and emotional energy to turn the spotlight away from my husband and focused it on myself, I was convicted and humbled by what it revealed. There in its glare stood a woman who still enjoyed admiring looks from other men, and who felt a little less valuable when she didn't get them. The very thing I didn't want my husband to do with other women was the thing *I* enjoyed receiving!

As I began to trust God and Pat to take care of Pat, I found new freedom to focus on working on Marsha. Today that work continues. Each time I start to worry about what my husband thinks and feels when he's around attractive women, I remind myself that I'm powerless over him, but I *am* responsible for *me*. I love the way *The Message* says it in Matthew 7:1–5:

> Don't pick on people, jump on their failures, criticize their faults—unless, of course, you want the same treatment. That critical spirit has a way of boomeranging. It's easy to see a smudge on your neighbor's face and be oblivious to the ugly sneer on your own. Do you have the nerve to say, "Let me wash your face for you," when your own face is distorted by contempt? It's this whole traveling road-show mentality all

over again, playing a holier-than-thou part instead of just living your part. Wipe that ugly sneer off your own face, and you might be fit to offer a washcloth to your neighbor.

Wow. That smarts. So many of the ways we think, behave, and interact are nothing less than "ugly sneers" that need to be washed away. As you pick up your spiritual mirror and examine your face and heart, do you see any of the negative relationship patterns listed below? I know I do.

Nagging	Self-righteousness
Manipulation	Lying
Controlling	Gossiping
Anger/rage	Punitive
Sexually unavailable	Sloppy about appearance
Perfectionism	Emotionally unavailable
Jealousy	Judging
Resentment	Suspiciousness

Any and all of these relationship patterns interfere with intimacy and damage a marriage.

How about the ways we treat our emotional pain? What do you reach for when things go wrong, when someone lets you down, or you're having a bad day? Many of us reach for at least one of the behaviors listed below.

Overeating	Anorexia and/or bulimia
Overspending	Physical affairs
Flirting	Alcohol
Romance novels	Dependency on male approval
Emotional affairs	Sleeping through the day
Prescription drugs	Street drugs

Though space won't allow me to deal with all of the negative relationship and emotional behaviors, I will touch on a few.

Sexually Unavailable

When talking about their wives, two negative patterns that men refer to most often are emotional and sexual unavailability. Husbands need and long for our physical and emotional love and warmth, even though they often don't know how to ask for it (or sometimes how to show it themselves!).

A couple of days ago, Pat came home from presenting his Sexual Integrity seminar for men and said, "You know, I never cease to be surprised at the number of men who tell me that they haven't had sex with their wives for months or even years, and that their wives simply aren't interested."

A young woman whose husband had a long affair with another woman in their church told this story:

> After finding out about the affair, I was devastated. I felt so betrayed by both of them. I went away to a women's retreat and spent the weekend with other women and in time alone with God. During those two days, I felt convicted about how infrequently I had expressed to my husband a desire for sex, which set up a pattern of infrequent lovemaking for us. I had to go home and apologize to him and take responsibility for how that must have felt to him. I know that's no excuse for what he's done, but I know now that I let him down, too.

So many husbands tell Pat the same story Dean does, but often it's too late to change the script:

> Don't get me wrong, my first wife is a great lady, but she never met any of my needs for affection. She's not a toucher or a hugger, and we rarely had sex. I know she thinks I left her for Jeannie because I preferred a younger, prettier woman. But that's not it at all. I left her because I was hungry for intimacy and

> warmth. What I did was sin and I can't blame my wife
> or anyone else. My affair was about the holes in my
> heart; in order to feel good about myself, I wanted to
> be stroked, affirmed, and comforted by a woman. Jean-
> nie did those things, and in my sin, I went for it.

No, we are not an excuse for our husbands to sin, but so many men long for their wife's warmth and affection. If your husband could be one of those men, find out why your thermostat is set at cool. Talk to a counselor; explore your emotions. Poke around in the memories of your childhood. See if part of you is still frozen there. Determine what you need to do to turn up your emotional and sexual dial. Not only will *you* benefit from looking at your past, it may be the best marriage insurance you can buy.

Anger

Christian author Nancy Groom says, "Anger that is un-acknowledged doesn't go away. It goes underground. And someone always pays."[4]

Does your anger ever spew forth from some underground reservoir you hoped had been drained? Mine does. I've had to do a lot of work on my anger, following its stream to a long-ago past. God and I will probably be draining it for the rest of my life. But however much work it takes, it's worth it. I've experienced firsthand the hurt and damage undrained anger can do.

Whether it's anger, an explosive temper, or the bitter bile of resentment, these relationship styles can poison a relationship. When we begin to change our attitude and use healthier communication styles, we alter our side of the marriage equation, which introduces change in the dynamic between us.

Alcohol

Although it doesn't show through their Sunday smiles, there are women—and men—who love and serve God, yet they've developed addictions to soothe their pain. Sharon Hersh, a Christian writer and counselor, told about her battle with alcoholism on our radio broadcast a few months ago.

> Early in marriage I began to experience panic attacks. Back then they didn't know a whole lot about panic attacks . . . and so the physician I saw said, "Well, why don't you just drink a glass of wine before you go to bed at night." So rather than looking at what was going on in my internal world with the panic and the debilitating fear and anxiety, I learned, just numb it. Make the pain go away.
>
> I think what is involved in every addiction, and certainly in mine, is a desire to escape from the realities of life. One fourth of all women who struggle with addictions do have some sort of trauma in their pasts. And when God was gracious enough to help me begin to understand what was going on, I found that there were years of not looking at trauma and pain and a sense of betrayal from others, as well as my own sinful choices, that I wanted to escape from. For me, alcohol was the perfect way to do that.
>
> This was all going on while I was a Christian and very active in our church. I was in charge of children's ministries and my husband was the head of the deacon board.

Some of us avoid the "bad" things like alcohol, and use the comfort of more respectable things, like food, to medicate our feelings.

Overeating/Eating Disorders

I don't know about you, but for me, food is the easiest and most socially acceptable drug of all. If I'm down, I open the refrigerator door; if I'm lonely, I open the refrigerator door; in fact, when I feel any negative emotion, the place I automatically go is that big cold box full of available temptations. I can hate myself tomorrow when I step on the scale first thing in the morning. Right now, I need to feel better.

How can food get this much power? Because it momentarily soothes and medicates our feelings. Just as Sharon was powerless over alcohol, those of us who use food for comfort are powerless as well, and must surrender that weakness to God if we want freedom. For some of us, using food to numb pain mutates into anorexia and bulimia, destroying our lives and our bodies. Author Cynthia Rowland McClure was one who fought this disorder, and with God's help, she finally won. She talks about the power our addictions have when they remain a secret.

> To me, this is the saddest part of the monster bulimia. It's a secret addiction. Whom do you tell? I was on television reporting the news; do you really think I'd tell someone, "Hey, I'd like you to know I eat ten candy bars at a time and pop sixty to one hundred laxatives a day!" No way! Bulimia is a completely embarrassing disorder. Your life becomes a toilet, and few people desire to reveal that secret, least of all me. I always had known that if I did reveal my monster within me I would certainly be rejected.[5]

Sleeping through the Day

More than one woman has told me she uses sleeping to avoid feeling her pain. This is Rene's story:

> Living with my husband's addiction hurt so much I couldn't stand it. I wanted to run, but I had children

and I didn't know where we could go. I felt so trapped. I wasn't working when the kids were in grade school, so after they left for school in the morning, I took sleeping pills, set the alarm clock for 2:00 P.M., and slept the day away so I wouldn't have to feel. When the alarm went off, I got up, smoothed the bed, fixed my hair and makeup, and was ready to pretend when everyone came home. Now I realize that this was a sort of addiction because I was treating my pain instead of confronting the situation. It was wrong, and a terrible waste.

It takes courage, but we must resist the temporary anesthesia of these avoidance behaviors, and, instead, directly confront our problems.

Emotional Affairs

Often a woman who doesn't get all her emotional needs met in her marriage tries to connect with another man on an emotional level, disregarding the fact that she—and possibly he—are married. But emotional intimacy between a man and a woman is a precious bond reserved for a husband and a wife. When a third person wedges into that bond, she is placing herself where she has no business; what she's doing is not fair to her spouse, the other man, or to the other woman.

Recently a friend told me this story through eyes filled with tears:

My husband's secretary and I had been friends for years. I had no idea that the two of them had become emotionally involved until he came to me one day three years ago and told me he wanted a divorce so he could marry her. He told me—and, knowing him, I believe him—that they had not had sex because they wanted to keep their love pure until after they were married. But he said they knew they were deeply in love. It didn't hurt any less to know they hadn't had a sexual relationship. Just knowing he had been emotionally intimate with another woman broke my heart. How could they do this to me?

Many Christian women intentionally play with men's emotions by complimenting, admiring, and seeking "spiritual counsel," all with the purpose of getting an emotional hit. But this is emotional adultery and can lead to physical adultery. As Christian women, we have no business playing this game.

Romance Addiction

Emotional and physical affairs are a form of romance addiction—the feeling that love and comfort and excitement will add the missing ingredients to our lives. One way we as women act this out includes compulsively reading romance novels. The following letter recently ran in the *Focus on the Family Magazine with Dr. James Dobson:*

I hear so many warnings about pornographic magazines, pornography on the Internet, etc. But what about the so-called "romance novels"? These books are sexually explicit, they contain violence of a sexual nature, and they are also addictive.

There was a time when I couldn't put them down. I had a tendency to shut out my family and ignore my responsibilities.

I read this material for years before, and after, becoming a Christian. It caused problems in my relationships and my marriage. My husband hauled the novels out of our home by the box full.

I thought I was the only person with this problem. But recently I have found others, and it is causing problems for them too.

Lynda Kline, Prescott, Arizona[6]

Lynda is undoubtedly describing secular romance novels, yet even *compulsive* reading of Christian ones can be used to avoid our true feelings.

Cynthia Rowland McClure advises us about this romance hunger we feel.

> I encourage you to find out why you need an unhealthy relationship. Some of you are looking for the dad you never had; some of you are in abusive relationships because you feel you deserve to be abused; some of you are looking for love through sexual intimacies, because your dads may have never hugged you or the relationship was never emotional or maybe your parents never said out loud, "I love you."[7]

Getting in touch with *what* we feel is the first step. Then we need to explore *why* we feel emotional pain, and to recognize what it is we reach for to treat it. Is it food, shopping, flirting, addiction to romance novels, prescription drugs, or something else? If we work to eliminate those behaviors and the pain behind them, we are better equipped to handle the trauma our husbands' sexual sin has delivered into our lives. By recognizing our weakness, we can avoid reaching for our own addictive behaviors and instead reach out to God and others to help us through the pain in our marriages.

The Need for Support

Changing timeworn habits is extremely difficult and close to impossible without support. Trying to do it alone—especially during a marriage crisis—usually breeds more discouragement. A counselor or a loving support group makes all the difference. When we let our counselor or group take part in our growth, we gain accountability partners to reinforce our progress. And with accountability comes their prayers, understanding, grace, and cheers of encouragement.

Recently, an old friend from California visited me, and we spent several hours at a beachfront park. Late in the day, we sat on a bench near the water's edge and bathed in the long, low rays of the afternoon sun. For a few minutes, we just sat there, lazily taking in the layers of beauty before us—the blue water, the sailboats, the nearby San Juan Islands, and the Olympic Mountains in the distance. Eventually our conversation turned to the subject of support groups. We reflected on how learning to be deeply honest can bring both joy and stark terror. My friend went on to share an example of a secret behavior she used to practice, but had been freed from through involvement in her group.

> Even though I was married, I used to need affirmation from men to know that I was worthwhile. I would spend lots of time getting fixed up to look my best and then go to stores and pretend to shop, just to get admiring looks from men. But once I got in a support group that held me accountable, I couldn't get away with it anymore. The group held me responsible for the growth I said I wanted in my life. And it's worked. Now it's so wonderful to be free from that insatiable need to know I'm okay. As I've faced the truth about myself and spoken it out loud to other women who give me unconditional love, encouragement, and accountability, I've learned that the more open and honest I am, the more God can do his work through me.

The kind of change my friend made doesn't happen without accountability. She was part of a group that confronted her and held her accountable for her actions when she did things she had told them she wasn't going to do anymore. To let ourselves become that vulnerable, that transparent, we have to make a decision to prioritize growth, find a group that will hold us accountable, then follow those steps with lots of hard work and prayer. Even then, the other people in our lives might not change just because we do. Ultimately the only person we can change is ourselves. And we can't change the past—the bad memories, the people that hurt us, or the wrong things we've done. But we can confront the memories and understand how things hurt us, and we can take responsibility for the wrong things we've done. And then we can ask forgiveness.

In his perfect love, our heavenly Father places in our hands the beautiful gift of forgiveness. Don't hesitate to open this gift. Don't wonder if you have done enough to earn it. Don't question your right to possess it. He is your Father, and your repentant heart is all he needs to give it to you. Wear his gift—the glorious garment of forgiveness— with your head held high, and with the pleasure that comes from knowing you do look your best, because you are a beautiful child of God.

7

The Healing Power of Making Amends

"I Love You" Means Saying You're Sorry

> When a man or woman wrongs another in any way
> and so is unfaithful to the LORD, that person is guilty
> and must confess the sin he has committed. He must
> make full restitution for his wrong.
>
> *Numbers 5:6–7 NIV*

"I just can't see our situation ever changing," Mark said softly, letting out a long and heavy sigh. His words filled the darkness in the bedroom, and hung there between them, creating a wall as they had so many times before.

Oh, not again, Ginger thought. She could barely see the outline of his head on his pillow but she knew too well the look on his face. She felt grateful that she couldn't see his eyes. She always felt pangs of guilt and deep frustration when she saw the sadness that shadowed them when he talked about his lost dreams. *Why can't he just deal with it and let it go? Isn't twenty years long enough to carry something?* They both knew that now with children to raise and great financial pressure, it would take a miracle to make his dreams a reality.

"I've known most of my life that God called me to the ministry and now I've been stuck in a dead-end job for twenty years," Mark said. "I feel like I've wasted my life. I want to do something meaningful and now it feels like we'll be stuck forever."

Ginger told me what she felt that night:

> I don't know what shifted in me, but for some reason this time was different. I started to really listen to Mark. You know, it was the first time since we've been married that I really heard—with my heart—what he was saying. It was the first time I'd ever been able to step inside his skin and feel a little bit of what that must have been like for him to lose his dreams because of my illness. And I knew, way down inside—for the first time—how much I had really hurt him. Genuine tears of regret spilled out and wet the pillow by my cheek. Suddenly it didn't matter anymore if I was right or wrong—what mattered was that ministry was the one thing that Mark had felt called to do with his life. And I had no right to judge that.

"I'm *really, really* sorry, Mark," Ginger responded. "I'm really sorry for how my breakdown and all those years of my emotional pain forced you to give up your dreams, and how I was so wrapped up in myself, I couldn't see you. And I'm really sorry that for all these years I've minimized the pain and loss that my stuff has caused you." Ginger went on to explain to me:

> You know, what's interesting about my amends making that night is that Mark wasn't able to accept it right away, but it didn't matter, I was free of it. I don't

have any more amends to make for it; I don't have any more excuses to offer for it—I'm free of it because I finally made my amends to him, and for me and God, it's resolved. I don't have to carry it around anymore. There'll be other things I'll have to make amends for, but that's not one of them.

Now Mark is making amends to me for the ways his sexual addiction has hurt me and our relationship. Each of us is making amends to the other for those wounds. It's a quiet thing, but it's really powerful. There's a new softness over our relationship now. It's really wonderful.

The Who, What, and Why of Making Amends

Making amends means taking responsibility for our attitudes and actions that have hurt other people. And this includes our husbands. It may take time before we feel ready to follow Ginger's example and take this difficult step in our own spiritual journey. And it will be especially hard if your husband is involved with another woman and doesn't care about saving the marriage. Right now he may seem to be the "enemy." After all, he is the one responsible for the deep pain you feel. When our husbands are involved in any kind of inappropriate sexual behavior, the thought of accepting responsibility for our own "minor transgressions" in the marriage may sound unthinkable and ridiculous. It may feel like we're being asked to give ourselves away. We may still be filled with resentment and not ready to take this step. That's okay. God can meet us where we are; he can walk with us through the grief and anger and still be with us when we're ready to make amends.

When we are ready, when it's God's time, taking this difficult step will strengthen our own spiritual lives, and God may use it to reopen communication with our husbands, and possibly to bring healing to our marriages. Taking this step requires a willingness to honestly examine ourselves. Dr. Jennifer Schneider, whose husband was a sex addict, made amends to him as a part of strengthening her own spiritual life. She shares her insights about this important step:

> Making amends first requires facing the truth about the effects of our behavior on other people. Did our critical attitude cause those around us to feel defensive? Did our need to control cause resentment by those we tried to control? Did our irresponsibility make others have to do our work for us? Did we hurt another woman by our unjustified jealousy? . . . Making amends to others is painful; it takes courage and humility. But the result is an increased sense of self-worth and peace of mind. The objective of making amends is to accept personal responsibility for our past behavior.[1]

We make amends not only to accept personal responsibility for past behavior, but more importantly, we do it to clear our relationships with others, particularly with our husbands, because we recognize that our own actions and motives in the marriage haven't always been pure. If doing so reopens communication with our husbands and leads to healing our marriages, we are grateful, but that isn't our initial and primary reason for making amends. Rather, it is to clear, as completely as we know how, our relationship with God. It's our opportunity to sweep *our* side of the street so we'll know we've done everything God requires of us.

Florence, whose twenty-four-year-long marriage has weathered many storms, has learned the relational value of making amends.

> For me, making amends in any relationship opens up a blockage that keeps it from going where it could go. I know that in my own marriage when I hold back on wrongs I've done, it interferes with my intimacy

with Dan. Somehow clearing the air and bringing something I've done—even if it's a secret—out into the open has a way of drawing us closer. I would say those amends-making times are our most intimate. Often, we're lying in bed at night before we go to sleep and an issue or incident comes up—something one of us has done to the other that was hurtful—and we make amends, and it's just so healing. And the reward of it—I set out to do it because I need to for myself, but what comes back from Dan is a new tenderness. It helps him trust me more, too, because he sees I'm being more honest. Usually my wrongdoing is something he already knows about because it hurt him, but by acknowledging my guilt and asking for his forgiveness, his respect for me increases. The rewards come back in so many ways.

Making amends requires humility, and for that reason it takes courage. The words, "I was wrong. I'm really sorry. Will you forgive me?" look simple on paper, but they can get stuck in my throat. I've found that if I think about it for too long, I can talk myself out of making amends. But when I just do it and trust God with the results, I feel better about the kind of person I am, my walk with the Lord remains fresh, and my self-respect grows.

My friend Marcie explains the tie she feels between amends and self-respect.

When I initially contemplate making amends and then follow through and make them, I feel really awful—I'm so aware of my sin nature and how I let it enter into the way I treat others. I think, *How's this person going to react when I talk about it? How will he interpret it?* Even though I take this step because I need to, it's really hard not to worry about the other person's reaction. I wonder if that person is still going to

love me. I'm always amazed when it draws the relationship even closer because in my mind, I'm only
aware of my guilt. I feel better about myself when I'm
finished, even if the other person doesn't accept my
amends. I know in my heart that I've done what God
wants me to, and he's forgiven me.

As hard as it is to swallow our pride at times, Marcie is
right when she says, "I know in my heart that I've done what
God wants me to." In Romans 12:18 we are told, "If it is
possible, as far as it depends on you, live at peace with everyone" (NIV). The clear implication of this Scripture is that
our amends making may not produce complete reconciliation with the other person. But God simply wants us to do
our part, and to know that, ultimately, that is all we can do.

The Components of Amends Making

The word *amends* sounds dated, but when put to use in
human conflicts, its healing power rivals our most modern
antibiotics. Injected into unforgotten transgressions, its
potent serum can kill the relational maladies of anger,
resentment, and long-held pain.

Apology

The movie *Love Story* defined love as, "Never having to
say you're sorry." But in real-life relationships, "I'm sorry"
is a requirement if we want wounds to be healed and hearts
to be mended. So the first part of making amends is simply saying those magic words you were taught as a child:
"I'm sorry. Will you forgive me?"

Restitution

The second step of amends making is restitution. As we
make amends, David Augsburger cautions us to remember

that "the focus is not on *asking* for something but on *demonstrating* repentance. I can go to the one I have injured and say, 'I have injured you. I recognize that. I deeply regret what I have done.'"[2]

We follow up with a statement such as, "What can I do to make this right?" Often there is nothing tangible that can be done to undo a past wrong, but we need to give the other person the chance to make that judgment. We need to be willing to try to set things right.

The Right Attitude

As hard as it may be, we must focus only on ourselves. I find the hardest part of amends is leaving the other person's wrongs out of it. Like me, you may feel tempted to tack on, "You know, if you hadn't done what *you* did, I never would have acted the way *I* did!" But if we give in to this temptation, it's no longer a true apology because we haven't owned our guilt. It's just more excuse making. We need to willingly admit our faults and leave the results to God as we try to make peace between our husbands and ourselves.

Dotty has learned how important attitude is in this process.

> I don't go into it unless it's 100 percent owning my part with no thought of what that other person has done to me. There've been times when I knew I needed to make amends, but I still felt very aware that the other person did wrongs, too. That means I'm not ready to make amends because a little part of me is still hanging onto the other person's wrongdoing. There've been times when I put off making amends for a long time because I didn't want to go into it that way and I didn't feel ready to do it right. I knew the other person would be able to feel that little part I was hanging onto and it would cancel out the amends. I wanted it to be total 100 percent owning of my stuff with no thought of what

> that other person did. It's hard, but that's the only way to make it *my* amends.

There's a second way that a wrong attitude can present itself. Sometimes the person we're apologizing to will try to make us feel better by attempting to minimize what we've done to hurt them. If, in response to your amends, your husband or someone else says, "Well, you did what you did because of my failure. You had a right to be angry," don't say, "You know, you're right. I wouldn't have done that if it wasn't for what you did to me." Instead, say, "Right now it's time for me to take responsibility for my behavior." Not only will your spiritual cup be washed clean, your husband will feel freer to consider *his* actions and their impact on the marriage.

Doing No Harm

Like the physician's creed, we should "First do no harm." If we will hurt someone else by making our amends, we need to stop, think, and pray about it. Yet we also need to be careful not to use this as an excuse to keep our sinful secrets. Like so many things in the Christian walk, we must turn to God for guidance and perhaps seek counsel from our pastor or another mature Christian.

Using Whatever Means We Have To

I've known people who made long trips to make amends face-to-face. I've known others who chose to offer their amends in a letter. Again, look to God for direction on how best to handle each situation. Actions that occurred long ago with a sister or brother who may live on the other side of the country will likely require a different approach than a fight you had with your husband last week. The following format, adapted from *If Only You Would Change*, may be helpful.

1. I want to fully admit my responsibility for the ways I have hurt you in the past. (List your hurtful actions and attitudes. Write your direct amends down word for word, exactly as you plan to say it. Be brief and to the point.)
2. I am sorry for the many ways these actions have hurt you.
3. Please forgive me.[3]
4. Read over your direct amends a few days after you have written it. Be careful to eliminate any implication of blame toward the other person for your actions.
5. Present your amends.

Though the means may be a letter, a telephone call, or a face-to-face conversation, the process remains pretty much the same. We admit our guilt, take responsibility for it, ask for forgiveness, and ask what we can do to make it right.

Don't Procrastinate

Because owning our guilt out loud means losing face and/or possible rejection, procrastination crowds in alongside fear, and together they rope us to our failures, guilt, and broken relationships and try to shut the door between us and God. The things procrastination whispers in our ear can sound so sensible: "Well, let's just let bygones be bygones." Or how about, "I hurt him a little, he hurt me a little; let's just call it even." Procrastination even wraps its messages in spirituality, saying things like, "It's covered by the blood. As long as I've confessed it to God, it's taken care of."

Jody told me recently she is still trying to untie these ropes.

> Alex and I have been divorced for twelve years, and I still haven't had the courage to take complete responsibility for my failures in the marriage. He hurt me and the girls in so many ways—there was physical abuse and he was mean in other ways, too. But I

wasn't always perfect. I resented him deeply and sometimes I put him down, belittling his choices in life. Now that I've committed myself to a path of spiritual growth, I feel deep conviction, and I know it won't go away until I take full responsibility for my wrongs and make amends to Alex. I just keep procrastinating by maintaining my excuses: He's remarried and I shouldn't interfere in his new life. I've asked God's forgiveness and I know he's forgiven me, and besides, what if Alex doesn't accept my amends? But I know I won't have complete peace until I quit making these excuses and take the necessary step.

Are you, like Jody, letting your wrongs remain a part of your unresolved history? Ask God to bring to mind the ways you've hurt other people, then begin to pray and seek his direction on what you should do about it.

Overcoming Our Fears

What about the times when our fears of being rejected, scoffed at, or treated with anger come true? Romans 12:17 admonishes us, "Do not repay anyone evil for evil" (NIV). It's true that our amends may be rejected, but we will still have the peace that comes from following God's best for our life by sweeping our side of the street.

Ginger, who made amends to her husband as they lay in bed, adds this wisdom to the thoughts she shared earlier:

Even if someone resents me, as long as I've sincerely made my amends for it, I don't have to feel guilty anymore. It's like things are all sparkly and clean. Something has cleared inside. Keeping short accounts by staying current on my amends helps keep me grounded and more aware of when I say and do things that will require an amends later. It makes me more responsible for my behavior.

But usually our efforts of apology and restitution will find ready reception. You'll discover that most people will appreciate your contrite spirit and freely offer their forgiveness. And God often blesses our attempts at obedience by healing and restoring our relationships.

Forgiving Ourselves

Sometimes forgiving ourselves is the hardest task of all. I know from experience. Like most parents, I adore my children and loved watching them grow up, yet I made many, many mistakes along the way. Oh, to be able to go back and try again with the wisdom of hindsight. Since that's not possible, I wanted to try to take responsibility for my failures—those I was aware of and those I wasn't. So I wrote my son and daughter each a long letter, including the list of wrongs I could remember. Then I added another sheet of paper with only numbers and asked them to finish the list so I could take responsibility and make amends for the things I had overlooked or forgotten. In closing, I asked each of them to go to a counselor alone with me so we could try to resolve the hurts and damage my failures and wrong choices brought into their lives.

With hearts of love, they both covered my wrongs with blankets of forgiveness; they didn't fill in the blanks in my memory and passed on the counseling. But knowing my failure and well aware of my guilt, I felt like I needed more— to have them yell at me or something! Somehow, without their condemnation, I've found it difficult to accept their forgiveness.

Last week over iced tea, I talked to my friend Anita about my feelings. I appreciated her insights. Anita said:

> When I can't let go of my guilt, I need to deal with the residue myself and not cling to the person I offended, trying to wring more forgiveness from him or her. I need to learn to extend the same grace to

> myself that God extends to me. I need to recognize that I am a person worthy of giving myself second chances and of other people giving me second chances. I have to believe that there are people willing to do that. And at the same time, I'm always amazed when they are willing! I tend to feel like if I fail, it cancels out everything good about me.

I appreciated the reminder that God buries our sins in the deepest sea, and as Corrie ten Boom said, "He then puts a sign on the bank which says: 'No fishing allowed.'"

The Resulting Peace

When we've cleared our relationships with people and with God, these actions produce peace inside, because we know we have done our best to take responsibility for our failures. Natalie describes the peace she feels after making amends with someone:

> It has an incredible effect on me, when I make amends. In my next time with the Lord, either in reading or at church, I'll discover that there is another space that has opened up. It's like I can receive God in his fullness because I've made more space for him. There are times when it feels like he can only funnel a trickle into my heart. But when my heart is clean, it's like his fullness rushes in to fill me with more of himself because the connection between us is cleared. If I can keep working and make amends to keep things cleared, the rewards that come back are wonderful.

As we are obedient to sweep clean our side of the street, it frees up energy within us—energy that we'll need to face the next step in our healing process.

Grieving Your Loss, Healing Your Heart

Shattered Castle Walls

> There is an appointed time for everything.
> And there is a time for every event under heaven . . .
> A time to weep, and a time to laugh;
> A time to mourn, and a time to dance.
>
> *Ecclesiastes 3:1, 4 NASB*

Orange, red, and blue flames played tag behind the fireplace glass, surrounded by cool, white slabs of Italian marble. White brocade drapes hung in graceful folds from the wide windows that looked out on the sparkling bay. Everything in the living room—the plush white carpeting, the elegant camelback sofa, and the gleaming gold chandeliers—said that this was a home with money and stability. But as I sat watching Collette in her Queen Anne wingback chair, arms folded across her bosom as she rocked back and forth in self-comfort, and listened to her deep, heart-wrenching sobs filling the beautiful room, I knew that her stability had vanished and all the money in the world couldn't ease her pain. Her story spilled out with her tears.

> I feel completely engulfed by my emotions. At times the pain paralyzes me. I'll be standing in the kitchen wiping dishes, or driving my car, or in the middle of a conversation, when out of nowhere, I envision him with prostitutes and it stabs me like a knife in my heart. The hurt is a torment, and the shame—the shame locks me in my house in this small town where everyone knows my husband, the doctor. And now, after reading the newspaper, everyone also knows he was picked up by police in the red-light district of the nearest city.
>
> How could he do this? How is it possible that a man with a good reputation as a doctor, Christian, husband, and father could have lied to me and our children? How can I be married to such a hypocrite? How could he look me in the eye day after day for years, pretending to love me?

The grief and emotional agony a wife experiences when she discovers her husband's sexual misconduct overwhelms her and leaves her reeling. She feels unable to cope with the crumbling truth she thought her marriage stood on. As the pieces of her life fall around her, she feels as if her whole world is disintegrating, and she's helpless to hold it together.

Discovering emotional or physical infidelity is a form of death. You cherished and trusted this man enough to let him know you fully—emotionally, physically, and spiritually. Now that man has broken your sacred trust, and when he did, something died. You can no longer turn to him with the certainty that he will value and protect the intimacy you shared. You can no longer go to him, knowing that when others reject you, he will still hold you precious and dear. Your loss is real and it slices your soul.

Through eyes clouded with pain, one woman told me, "It would have been easier if he had just died. At least then I wouldn't feel like a fool. I wouldn't have to live with the knowledge that he broke his commitment to me—that he betrayed me when I trusted him."

When we experience such a significant loss, we are thrown into the grief cycle, not unlike what happens when someone we love dies. Your grief is real and it won't be ignored; it will shred your emotions, ravage your world, and swallow your joy. Trying to hold in this much emotional pain only drains our energy. If we are ever to heal, grief demands we acknowledge it and, as painful as it is, embrace the grieving process.

Facing Your Grief

For many, the word *grieving* carries negative connotations. But to grieve simply means to face your losses, to let yourself feel the pain. Our friend, author and counselor Dr. Daryl Quick, wisely says, "You can't heal what you don't feel." But willing yourself to feel that grief may be the hardest thing you've ever done in your life. When I met Patricia, she had been holding her grief in for several months. She finally let herself feel it as we talked. As she did, she clung to me, her head on my shoulder, and wept, not wanting to let go.

Though grief arrives with a vengeance, it is not our enemy. It offers the only healthy way to work through our loss. Experiencing grief doesn't mean you have no faith; just the opposite is true. God gave us the ability to grieve to help heal our broken hearts.

125

The Bible and Grieving

Grieving is actually a wonderful biblical mandate. The second of Jesus' Beatitudes says, "Blessed are those who mourn, for they shall be comforted" (Matt. 5:4 NASB). Or, as *The Message* translates that verse: "You're blessed when you feel you've lost what is most dear to you. Only then can you be embraced by the One most dear to you." And Psalm 34:18 tells us, "The LORD is close to the broken-hearted, and saves those who are crushed in spirit" (NIV).

God cares about our grief and our broken hearts. We read that Jesus himself experienced grief just as we do. John 11:32–37 tells us that when his good friend Lazarus died, Jesus himself wept, and when he saw the others weeping, he was "deeply moved in spirit and troubled" (v. 33 NIV).

We are also told that God is present in our grief and comforts us, and that through our own grief, we learn to care about the grief of others and how to comfort them as well. Second Corinthians 1:3–4 says, "Praise be to the God . . . of all comfort, who comforts us in all our troubles, so that we can comfort those in any trouble with the comfort we ourselves have received from God" (NIV).

Grief is a part of being alive on this earth. It is also a process that takes time and needs to unfold naturally. But we can't do it alone; to grieve completely, we need solace and support along the way.

Sharing the Pain

How can we deal with our pain and loss? We need to share it with others. Ecclesiastes 4:9–10 tells us, "Two are better than one . . . For if either of them falls, the one will lift up his companion. But woe to the one who falls when there is not another to lift him up" (NASB). Each time we tell our story in a safe environment and relive what happened, the pain loses some of its power. Turn to a friend you know you can trust or to a counselor. Find a support group. But don't try to bear this burden alone. During a phone call, a woman named Suzanne told me how a true friend helped her:

> Donna, a Christian friend, was the one person who was there for me when my husband finally moved out after many affairs. When so many others turned away or just didn't know what to say, Donna stuck with me. She walked with me through the dark times, never judged me, but accepted me right where I was. This was five years ago, but she remains a dear and trusted friend to this day.

Jackie, who made it through the discovery of her husband's pornography addiction with the help of a support group, now leads a group for other wives in similar situations. I asked her what word of encouragement she could give to other women just beginning that painful journey. Jackie says:

> Know that you are not alone. You may feel alone, but you aren't. There are so many of us who have been down this road before you, and I encourage you to reach out for help. Call someone—a friend, a pastor's wife, or find a support group. Don't try to do this on your own; reach out for help!

If the group you need isn't available, consider a bereavement group; though the people there are grieving the death of a loved one, your grief is similar. You, too, have experienced a significant loss. To locate some kind of grief and loss group, ask your pastor, a counselor, or call your local crisis line. Hospitals and funeral directors may also be able to help you in your search. Getting support and working through your grief is absolutely essential for your emotional, spiritual, and even physical well-being.

Dr. Dean Ornish, a renowned heart doctor, believes there is a strong connection between love, intimacy, health, and healing. A five-year study was recently conducted with cancer patients. Part of those in the study group joined a support group, and part didn't. At the end of five years, the results showed *three times* as many deaths and *twice* as many cancer recurrences in those who hadn't been part of a support group. Dr. Ornish believes that "anything that takes you out of the experience of being separate is healing."[1]

The Emotional Cycle

When living with grief, expect your reeling emotions to cycle all over the place. First comes shock, then denial: "No, this can't be true!" Anger soon follows; next your brain bargains with reality, only to be overtaken with plummeting depression. Sometimes violence even visits, and normally rational women try to punish their husbands for their transgressions. One grieving—and very angry—wife told me, "It's a good thing we don't have a gun in the house." When feelings are this strong, they become dangerous, and we *must* seek professional help to deal with them in a healthy way.

"With or without violence," says Dr. James Dobson, "the hostility of this terrible ordeal is ventilated in a period of wrath, ending in physical and emotional exhaustion. Then a brief time of acceptance occurs, after which grief and sorrow return like an unwelcome visitor who so recently came to call. Finally, the cycle repeats itself on a revolving merry-go-round of misery."[2]

This "merry-go-round of misery" is jammed with a wide spectrum of feelings—feelings as different as apathy and rage. You may identify with many of the feelings described in the next section. You may have even experienced all of them in one day!

Feelings That Come with Grief

Denial	Confusion
Hurt	Rejection
Anger	Betrayal
Hate	Guilt
Loneliness	Resentment
Numbness	Hopelessness
Feeling lost	Suicidal thoughts
Fear	Obsessed with what he's done
Depression	Apathy
Love	Shock
Jealousy	Despair
Self-doubt	Exhaustion
Relief	Embarrassment
Rage	Physical pain

Whether or not you have experienced every emotion on this list, you will certainly experience many, and your feelings will recycle themselves as they vary in intensity.

Rejection

Margaret, a wife whose husband had many affairs and finally left her, is now a counselor helping other women through the grief she knows so well. She offers perspective gained from working with many women:

> Often I hear, "If only I were prettier and thinner, maybe he wouldn't be doing these things." And I tell them, "It's not about you. He made those choices, and all the 'If onlys' in the world won't change it." And then I work to help them get better.
>
> In the beginning, I help them plan each of the days between our appointments. Initially, they are in so much pain, we literally have to list "get up and shower,

fix my hair, and put on makeup," and on through the activities that normally come naturally. I also give them a "blessing bag," a bag in which they put a blessing they received somewhere during each day. It may only be that someone smiled at them on the street, or a friend called to see how they were doing. Then I have them bring the bag in to our next session. We dump out the bag's blessings and I ask her to read them. The first week there may be only seven, the second fourteen, but as the weeks pass, the blessings multiply. I also encourage a woman to dump out her blessings and read them when she gets blue, and to think of them as her little candlelights. It helps her to see that in the midst of her darkness, there are still rays of hope and light.

Betrayal

When I met Sue, her feelings of betrayal were still fresh and the pain of deceit still new. She told me how she discovered her husband's pornography addiction after they had been married for twenty-nine years:

Austin often took a long time in the bathroom getting ready in the morning and before going to bed at night. Although it irritated me when we were first married, I had gotten used to this pattern and didn't think too much about it after all these years. Then one night last winter, I woke up at 2:00 A.M. and Austin wasn't in bed with me. I got up and tiptoed through the dark house and saw light coming out of the downstairs bathroom door, which wasn't latched. I'm not sure why I didn't say anything before I opened the door—I guess I was curious about what was going on. I pushed the door open, and there stood Austin, masturbating while he looked at a pornographic magazine. I was devastated and enraged all at the same time. This man that

> I slept with was fantasizing about all those beautiful, naked women. Our sex life had never been the way some of my friends describe theirs, but to fall to this level and to betray me in this way? We've been on a roller coaster ever since.

You feel deceived. You have been. You may feel as if you don't even know your husband. You don't. You've discovered that your husband has been living a double life—the life you *thought* you had, and a life that is radically different. For some couples, the double life has been going on since before they were married—five, ten, twenty, even thirty or more years.

Confusion

When they first discover their husband's problem, many women don't know what to do—or even what they *want* to do. Earlier in the book, you met Earl and Sandy Wilson. The Wilsons are the authors of the book *Restoring the Fallen*, which tells about Earl's long-term sexual addiction and their restoration as a couple. Sandy talked about the emotions she felt when she learned about Earl's problem.

> I felt a lot of confusion about what was the right thing to do. One day I wanted to run, and the next day I wanted to stay. So I was really up and down for probably a full year. I finally made a decision to stay in the marriage because I had seen real evidence on his side that he was working on his issues.

Conflicted feelings and fears confuse us and create questions we may not know how to answer. It's important not to act on those early, raw feelings but instead to sort them out over time.

Vulnerability

Not only do we *feel* vulnerable in these marital situations, we *are* vulnerable. We're vulnerable to more hurt, to new discoveries about our husbands' addiction, vulnerable to the judgment of others, to financial insecurity, and to continued pain. Deceit in one area spreads mistrust like a cancer through every aspect of our relationship. After discovering her husband's ten-year-long addiction to pornography, Ally said to me, "I feel vulnerable in every way . . . even in the area of money. He lied to me for all those years. How do I know he's not lying to me about money, too?"

Depression

Sometimes the hurt aches so much we're certain we can't go on. Depression becomes a constant companion, coloring our world in blacks and deep grays. Some women lose interest in life, quit answering the telephone, and don't want to get out of bed in the morning. Often we can't concentrate, remember things, or make decisions. We isolate from others, feel exhausted, and sometimes just stare into space. Sleep won't come and hope fades. We feel lonely, helpless, without a future.

One woman's despair was so deep that she told me, "The affair was a very tough thing for me. I prayed that God would let me die. I just didn't want to live. I hurt so bad. I would say the toughest part was not having someone—being all alone."

And another woman's grief finally won. Her husband had been having affairs for several years, yet she stayed in the marriage, living with her pain. Then one day her philandering husband came home and found her slumped over his desk; she had taken her own life, unable to live with her grief any longer.

If you find yourself unable to cope and you experience symptoms of withdrawal or depression, talk with a professional counselor, pastor, or someone who will help you work through it. The risk involved in not sharing your pain is simply too great. Your doctor may recommend you take some type of medication temporarily to help you through the hardest time.

A Need for the Truth

Many women express a need to know the details of their husband's sexual transgressions. One pastor's wife who is a good friend of mine said:

> I had to know the details. I needed to know how the other woman compared to me. And I wanted to know other personal details about their sexual experience. I felt that if I was ever going to consider forgiving, I had to know what it was that I was forgiving.

And Lisa, another pastor's wife, told me:

> My personality is the type that wants to face the pain head-on. I wanted to deal with it. I pretty much wanted to know what the affair was about. I questioned Brian to death. I felt that if he told me some of the awful stuff of the affair, it was breaking the secret—the secret between him and the other woman. By telling me, it wasn't their secret anymore. But that was my personality, and I know as I talk to other women, that's not always the case.

The night we interviewed the Wilsons, Sandy told us about the pain of later discovering that there was more to Earl's story than he had originally told. Earl had initially confessed part of his history of sexual sin to Sandy. But the spiritual care team that shepherded the Wilsons through their three-year restoration felt there was more. They urged Earl to write a letter to Sandy and tell her the entire story of his sexual transgressions. Sandy described the pain she felt when reading the letter:

> When I read the letter it was like reinjury. Devastating. You think it's going to be just a little bit of stuff but you really have no idea. For me it would have been better if I had found out all at one time. It was much harder this way. There was so much lack of trust. I felt like, "Well, have you told it all, or tomorrow or next week are we going to hear more?"

On the show, Pat asked Sandy what she would say to a man who is afraid to share the whole story all at once, for fear his wife will leave him. Sandy paused a moment, then replied:

> I understand his fear, but every time a man tells more of the story it's such a reinjury, it's as fresh as the first time. It's like you take a knife and you stab her not once but over and over and over again. I would rather hear it all at once and know that I won't be hit with more later.

For the wife who needs to know, a husband should bravely sweep the corners clean through a complete confession, so that with God's help and loving support, his wife's trust can begin to grow again. But it's very important that such a confession is not done without support. These issues are too explosive and far too painful to be endured without a trusted mentor present to provide comfort and counsel for the wife who is about to hear information that may overwhelm her.

Obsession with the Details

Sometimes the need to know passes over a line and becomes an obsession. Even after a husband has told his wife everything, she is unable to believe him. She becomes stuck in a cycle of accusations and wants to know "the rest of the details." A wife caught in this pattern needs help, probably from a trained Christian counselor. She needs to process those stuck feelings and release them so she can continue moving through the grieving cycle toward healing. When describing this obsessive pattern, Dave Carder, author of *Torn Asunder,* says, "If left uncontrolled, it will eventually thwart the marriage from getting back on track."[3]

Anger

Anger plays a key role in the grieving process. If your husband has betrayed you through sexual misconduct, your anger is justified. It's a normal human emotion in response to the betrayal you've experienced. Some Christians wrongly believe that all expressions of anger are sinful. But Ephesians 4:26 says, "In your anger do not sin" (NIV). In other words, some ways of expressing anger are sinful, and others are not. Five verses later, the apostle Paul itemizes some of the sinful ways of expressing anger. Anger is wrong when it is characterized, Paul says, by "bitterness," "rage," "slander," and "malice" (4:31 NIV). But on the other side Carder says:

> During the anger phase following disclosure, don't hold back your hurt and anger. You may think, *I can't kick a man when he's down,* but consider this: Your expressing legitimate anger in a non-retaliatory way does not constitute "kicking" him; you're just processing . . . correctly. . . . If your partner has had an affair and betrayed you and his wedding vows, you need to be angry. And you don't need to hold his hand when you express your true feelings.[4]

For many women, their anger expands to include anger at God. Elizabeth Harris, who now counsels other women, told her story on our broadcast. She was bravely honest when she talked about her anger after she discovered her husband's pornography addiction:

> I was very angry; I was angry at my husband, and I was angry at God. I was a Christian and I thought, "Where were you when this was happening?" And to be honest, I was angry at all the men on the earth.

Not only is anger normal and justified when expressed appropriately, it plays a key role in holding depression at bay. "Anger, strangely enough, helps keep the spouse out of the downward spiral of depression," says Carder. "Usually depression is the result of repressing or denying appropriate feelings of anger. In contrast, expressing anger helps keep the overwhelming, black feelings of depression away."[5]

Dr. Harry Schaumburg, the Denver counselor we quoted earlier, specializes in helping restore marriages torn by unfaithfulness. He warns against keeping anger's "raging torrents" deep inside:

> That isn't healthy. Deep-rooted anger can lead to sickness and many other problems. It's important for you to choose to deal with your anger constructively. One of the best ways to do this is to talk with an objective third person—your pastor, a counselor, a special friend—who will keep your confidence and be a good listener.[6]

We have all experienced the negative aspects of anger at some time. Among them are anger that refuses to wane in spite of time and repeated expression, anger that brings physical or emotional harm, and anger that wants to get even. Lynette, a woman whose husband frequented prostitutes, was unable to let go of her rage, even after giving it repeated expression. When her anger became physical, she knew she was out of control.

> I couldn't seem to quit badgering him. I couldn't quit asking "Why?" "How?" and "When?" Once I completely lost control and threw a thick book and a heavy ashtray at him, leaving big, purple bruises on his chest.

Lynette knew she was completely over the line into unhealthy behavior, and she reached out for help from her Christian counselor.

The Desire to "Get Back"

If we probe our hearts and find a desire to make our husbands hurt as we've been hurt, to make them pay, or to "get back" at them, then our anger is counterproductive.

Richard and Pam Crist have one of the most powerful testimonies we've ever heard. God restored their shattered marriage after years of sexual sin. As we shared earlier, Pam reached a period in her life when she finally became fed up with Rich's affairs and other sexual sins. She took the kids and moved out of state, though she later moved back home again. Rich was still involved in his sexual practices. In her pain and anger, Pam eventually retaliated, falling into some of the same sins Rich was still caught up in. On *Love Under Fire*, she gave us a vulnerably honest look into her heart during this time:

> I went home but not for the right reasons. I went home because I was still awfully angry, and bitter, and vengeful. So God had to make me realize that I was really no better than my husband. There were nights that I didn't come home; I was drinking and involved in immoral acts. My life was out of control—both our lives were out of control. I know now that you're not

> hurting the other person when you try to get back this way. The bitterness and anger only turn on yourself and your family. I tried to hurt him for what he'd done to me, but instead I hurt my kids, myself, and the testimony of Christ.

As counterproductive as Pam's retaliation was, vengeance isn't the only way to misuse anger. As psychologist Harriet Lerner says, "Those of us who are locked into ineffective expressions of anger suffer as deeply as those of us who are not getting angry at all."[7]

Some of us go the opposite direction and are *afraid* to let ourselves feel our anger, so we find ways to avoid it by throwing ourselves into our work, which can lead to workaholism. Others turn to their children to meet their emotional needs. This is one of the most damaging paths to take. It can lead to unhealthy enmeshment with them, and it forces them to try to meet your emotional needs. That's a huge burden for a child to bear, and it can create problems for them when they're young, as well as later in life.

Whatever feelings come up for us, we need to let ourselves *feel* them and work through them, including the anger, even though its power may frighten us. But we don't need to feel these emotions without support; no one can grapple with tsunami-sized emotions alone and expect to heal completely. Find a place where you will receive love, understanding, prayer, and commitment during your healing process.

An Encounter with Old Losses

As you do this grieving work, you may be surprised to bump into grief and loss from long ago. Because our present pain often taps into our life history and connects with emotional damage from the past, healing old hurts in our lives is frequently part of the process we must go through as we deal with our husbands' sexual betrayal. Mark Laaser, author of *Faithful and True* and a leading Christian expert in the sexual addiction field, believes that the spouse *must* do this work in order for the *couple* to heal.[8]

This was true for Margaret, the woman whose husband left her after years of affairs, and who is now a counselor helping other women. As we talked, Margaret explained the connection she'd discovered between her past and present pain.

> After he left, I got into counseling with a Christian therapist. Working with her played the major role in my healing. She helped me see the link between the abusive family I grew up in and my decision to marry an abusive man. I mean, Brandon had beaten me from the time we were dating! And then there were all his affairs after we got married. I think I put up with it all, and didn't confront him, because it all seemed so familiar. So I had a lot of behaviors and thought patterns from my past that needed to be changed before I could heal completely.

Janice is another woman I spent some time with, talking about how God finally healed her painful marriage. She told me she had the strength to deal with the present only after she had dealt with the past. Her husband was deep in sexual addiction of many kinds for thirty years of marriage, but Janice told me how she finally found the courage to leave him:

> I first discovered his sexual addiction several years after we were married. I confronted him and we separated three times during the next several years, but I always came back, even though he never made a commitment to change. It was only after I dealt with my childhood losses that I had the courage to leave

him and not come back until he changed. Before that, I was afraid, because we had three children to support and I wasn't sure I could make it on my own. When I finally dealt with the past, I became brave and took the kids and left. The last separation lasted until he finally came clean—thirty years after getting married.

Christian actress Carol Anderson's husband was involved in a homosexual lifestyle prior to their engagement, and she also fought anorexia and bulimia for twelve years. Carol tells how her childhood issues affected her adult relationships and habits:

As we got closer, he got more scared, and a lot of his struggles that were coming up he didn't discuss with me. I, on the other hand, though I didn't realize it, had a major codependency disorder. I had developed a pattern in my life of being attracted to men who were emotionally unavailable. Often I would date dangerous men. Even as a Christian, I would find the good guys kind of boring, and the exciting ones, the dangerous ones, the unavailable ones would be the ones I would be attracted to. Here I was again, in a different situation, but again with someone who wasn't available. He could be, but he was still dealing with too much of his homosexual struggle.

By the time we got engaged, Jim was having trouble with the fact that he was kind of leading a double life. When he finally told me about it, I listened and was so scared of losing him, was so afraid of being alone, I said, "Well that's okay; we'll work it out. Let's just keep the wedding date and we'll work it out."

But God had really put it on his heart to end the relationship. Which was a good thing, but at the time, it was the worst pain I'd ever been through. I felt rejected and abandoned. I had heard God say this was the man I would marry and I'm thinking, *Okay, are we hearing two Gods here?*

It forced me to go into counseling, which I thought I was doing just to get through the grief of the loss of my engagement, my dreams, and all that. What I actually ended up doing was spending a year addressing my father issues. I had to deal with the pain I felt because of my emotionally distant father. He was the guy who was never available for me, who couldn't respond, who couldn't embrace the need I had to be loved.

For years I had been trying to work out my father issues in unhealthy ways. I tried to fill the hole with my addiction to food and my compulsion about my weight. I also tried to work out my childhood issues through relationships with men. Whenever I could finally get an unavailable to fall in love with me, I would lose interest. The turnaround for me happened when I saw the connection between the hole inside me from having a dad who was never there, and my pursuit of unavailable men. When I finally began grieving the pain of not having what I needed with my earthly dad, I started the process of having God fill that need with himself.

Working through childhood pain while facing the hurt created by your husband's behavior is doubly hard, but often it is the only true path to healing ourselves and our marriages. Author Colette Dowling summarizes it well in her book, *Perfect Women*. She says, "It takes courage [to work on pain from our past]. It means facing the fact that others hurt us. Only then can we mourn the loss of those things we needed but were not given."[9]

As hard as it is, examining our hurt and learning how it shaped us illuminates these fragile places inside and teaches us what we need in order to heal.

The Road to Healing and Forgiveness

The road to healing takes time. Undoubtedly, you need time to grieve before you can even think about forgiving. Grieving isn't easy. Our losses are painfully real. Juanita Ryan's beautiful poem below describes the overwhelming grief we feel.

Shattered

It is lying all around me,
shattered into useless pieces of glass
that could now rip my unprotected feet.
It was the glass castle in which I lived
as fairy-princess and heroine-in-shining-armor,
ready and able to rescue all in need.
It was my fragile fantasy,
designed to protect me from the searing pain
of having never been rescued from my own unspeakable
distress.
But an invited enemy came
and rammed my castle doors, besieged my walls
and shattered my glass defense.
And so, what I once thought of as my castle-grand
is now nothing more than unrecognizable, jagged pieces.
And here I stand, exposed and stunned.
It is mine now, not to gather,
but to leave these shattered remains.
It is mine to find a way to live without this illusion.
It is mine to learn to be
the peasant child I am,
bereft of shining armor and magic wand.
But all I can see at this moment
are the broken pieces of my shattered castle walls.
And all I can do for now is weep.

— 9 —

Forgive and Forget?

From Resentment to Rose Petals

The difference between holding on to a hurt or releasing it with forgiveness is like the difference between
laying your head down at night on a pillow filled with
thorns or a pillow filled with rose petals.

Loren Fincher,
More Stories from the Heart

We were on the air one Friday night
doing our *Love Under Fire* show, when
we received a call that was especially
painful to listen to. I sat across the counter from Pat, head-
phones on, when the computer screen showed that we had
a caller named Roni. Pat punched the button that opens
the line between the broadcast and the caller, and said, "Hi,
Roni, you're on the air. How can we help you tonight?"
Through crying that sometimes turned to soft sobs, a young
voice told her story.

My husband is in the military; he's coming home
this weekend, and I just found out a couple of days
ago that he's been cheating on me overseas for the

143

last nine months. I knew nothing about the affair until two days ago when I got a call from the girl he's been with. She said her conscience wouldn't let her go without calling me and telling me what's been going on. I called my husband and confronted him on the phone, and he didn't lie. He said he's glad I know and that he wants to come home and work it out. I don't know where to start. My trust in him is gone, and my insecurities about myself as a woman are terrible right now. I was doing pretty well at first, but now I'm having a really hard time with it.

Roni is paying the high price of the marriage relationship, the uncertainty that comes with the intimacy package—the vulnerability to extreme pain and loss. When a woman glows in her moment as a bride, visions of radiant, glorious, everlasting love swirl in her heart and fill her mind. Bound by naivete, no one has told her that lust frequently lurks around the edge of most men's minds—even the minds of devout Christian men. The joy in her heart has bought off her reason, and she feels certain that in spite of the sexual temptations roaming the world around them, nothing can come between her and her man.

As brides, we're unaware or have chosen to forget that just beneath the words "I do" lies a price so high that paying it can feel like death itself. At the altar we've agreed to open our souls and our bodies to this man, though someday he may be disloyal or even betray us with sexual impurity. Lewis Smedes says that "anyone whose love dares to commit him is a candidate for forgiving. For when love commits you, it opens you up to hurts from people who go back on their commitments."[1]

So what is the price of marital union? It is the willingness to intimately connect with our husbands, knowing that betrayal is always a possibility. No matter how perfect and wonderful we think our man is, he, like us, remains human—

a fallible, fallen child of God. But the price of intimacy is worth it. And in spite of the pain, when our love mixes with our sin natures, the alchemy created produces rich personal growth, for it is within relationships that we do our best growing. Relationships present the perfect lab of life, and in this lab, a wife's first lesson should be to understand forgiveness: what it is, what it isn't, and how to do it.

What Is Forgiveness?

Two great Christian men stand out among others as modern-day apologists on the subject of forgiveness—David Augsburger and Lewis Smedes. Each is highly respected and extremely knowledgeable, yet even they don't agree on every point. Augsburger himself admits, "Christians have not always agreed about this."[2] If even great biblical scholars don't agree on every point about forgiveness, it's easy to understand why we sometimes feel confused.

Webster's New World Dictionary defines forgiveness this way: "to give up resentment against; stop being angry with; pardon; to give up all claim to punish or exact penalty for an offense; overlook; to cancel or remit a debt." And *Roget's Thesaurus* lists the following synonyms: "absolution, acquittal, exoneration, granting pardon, and reprieve."

I think that's an awful lot to ask from a woman whose husband has been physically, emotionally, or mentally unfaithful. And Lewis Smedes seems to agree when he says, "Forgiving seems almost unnatural. Our sense of fairness tells us people should pay for the wrong they do."[3]

For the Forgiven and the Forgiver

God in his great love for us created a relational paradox, for within the package of forgiveness waits a gift for both the forgiven and the forgiver. When we forgive someone, we ourselves are released from the resentments that eat our insides. God gives us the gift of freedom from the bitterness that can destroy our lives. As Smedes wisely puts it, when you forgive, "You set a prisoner free, but you discover that the real prisoner was yourself."[4] That sentence packs a powerful message. While our human nature wants to get even, God has something much better in mind. He wants to restore rest, peace, and joy to our lives.

What Forgiveness Isn't

Tolerating the Wrong

Some wrongly confuse forgiving an offender with tolerating or condoning the offense. The two are not the same. Scripture calls us to condemn the sin even as it points us toward forgiveness as our desired destination. This balance between condemning the wrongdoing while forgiving the offender is clearly illustrated in Jesus' encounter with the woman caught in adultery in John 8. After the woman's original accusers had each dropped their stones and filed out, Jesus asked the woman, "Hath no man condemned thee?" "No man, Lord," she replied. "Neither do I condemn thee," Jesus responded. "Go, and sin no more" (John 8:10–11 KJV). Jesus forgave the woman while labeling her behavior as sin and exhorting her not to do it anymore.

On the husband-wife level, this means there's room with forgiveness to release resentment while refusing to put up with the behavior itself.

Erasing the Past

Unfortunately, sexual impurity's impact on relationships can leave damage that even forgiveness can't erase. This was true for Earl and Sandy Wilson and their family, even though their children weren't young when Earl's sexual betrayal became public knowledge. Earl shared vulnerably on our radio broadcast:

> It was hard for our kids, too; as they heard more details, they didn't want to be around, because they were afraid they were going to hear more. . . . One of my sons said, "I don't know if I can ever love Dad again or if I can ever forgive him." Very hard words to hear, yet very appropriate from their point of view, because they had been very badly hurt.

And Sandy told how the kids' pain affected her, as well.

> One of the children blamed me. She said that if I'd been a better wife, this wouldn't have happened, and it was a long time before this turned around. I think she so badly needed a father that she needed to turn and be angry at me. It's been interesting to watch their growth during the years since then. She came home once and said, "I think I've decided it's not all your fault, Mom."

Even Earl's amends and Sandy's forgiveness can't undo all of the damage done by sexual impurity. Lewis Smedes says it very well:

Remember, you cannot erase the past, you can only heal the pain it has left behind. When you are wronged, that wrong becomes an indestructible reality. But you don't change the facts. And you do not undo all of their consequences. The dead stay dead; the wounded are often crippled still. The reality of evil and its damage to human beings is not magically undone and it can still make us very mad.[5]

Forgetting

Even though the phrase "forgive and forget" sounds spiritual, forgetting isn't necessarily a by-product of forgiveness, and we don't need to feel guilty when our memories remain. In fact, as David Augsbuger believes, "Forgetting tends to be a kind of sweet, pious denial blended with memory fatigue. You grow tired of remembering and you long once more to have a mind that is free from the review of the injury."[6] Forgiving isn't about forgetting. God didn't create our brains to work that way, but along with the ability to remember life's events, he promised to heal the pain sometimes contained in life's memories.

Ephesians 4:32 captures the simple essence of forgiveness. "And be kind to one another, tender-hearted, forgiving each other, just as God in Christ also has forgiven you" (NASB). The key to forgiveness is *not* forgetting, but rather *remembering*—remembering the many times Christ has forgiven us. With that remembering comes a humility that frees us to release the one who has hurt us. As Smedes says, "The really important thing is that we have the power to forgive what we still remember."[7] And what a beautiful miracle that is.

Why Forgive?

After discovering her husband's long affair with her best friend, one woman told me, "It's like we're in a tunnel of fire. If we can just make it through the tunnel, we might get out of the flames alive." But if we want out of the tunnel, if we want to experience freedom and peace, we must pay the fare—and that fare is forgiveness.

Why forgive? Smedes again has wise insight: "Forgiveness has the creative power to move us away from a past moment of pain," he says, "to unshackle us from our endless chain of reactions, and to create a new situation in which both the wrongdoer and the wronged can begin a new way."[8]

We forgive because we know that is what God wants for us. He wants us to be free from our bitterness. He wants us to know joy again. And he wants us to be able to continue to grow. He wants us to trade in our pillow filled with thorns for a pillow filled with rose petals.

But what do we do if we're just not ready to forgive? What do we do if we're somehow stuck? David Augsburger provides a wonderful answer to our question. He says, "Well, you can say something like, 'I, too, want forgiveness to be real between us. Can we work on it until we know that we've experienced it together.'"[9]

Forgiving Too Quickly

Sometimes we hurt so much we just want to get it over with and to go back to normalcy, so we forgive too quickly. We want to skip over all the work required to work through our painful feelings until we reach true forgiveness.

Our friend Jack McGinnis conducts grieving seminars in the United States and abroad and talks about the problem of forgiving too quickly. Jack is intimately acquainted with great loss and pain. His mother abandoned him and his alcoholic father when Jack was only five. As a little boy longing for a mother to love him, Jack would dial the operator and ask, "Can you find my mommy?" Late one night when Jack was ten, his dad lay drinking and smoking and dropped his cigarette. Unable to beat out the flames that developed, Jack watched in helpless horror as his father burned to death. During his remaining childhood years, Jack lived with unloving relatives, and his heart continued to ache for his mommy to love him. It wasn't until he was at midlife that Jack finally was helped to move through a grieving process for those childhood losses. During that time, he discovered the link between grieving and forgiveness. This is the way Jack explains that link:

> In order to complete the grieving of a loss, I have to come to the point of forgiving the person I hold responsible for the loss. Often, we are tempted to jump ahead to forgiveness before we have done our feeling work. The willingness to forgive is important, but if forgiveness is premature, it is not complete. I believe forgiveness comes at the end of the process, as a gift. The grieving system actually delivers forgiveness and somehow, in the process, God gives grace to forgive. What changes for me, then, is the way I carry the event or the person.[10]

Yet God doesn't abandon us if we're not ready to forgive. Deep hurt can take time to heal to the point of forgiveness. God can wait, and he'll walk with you as you struggle to reach authentic forgiveness. David's prayer to God in Psalm 51 reminds us that, above all else, God wants an *honest* response toward the one who has hurt us. David writes, "Surely you desire truth in the inner parts; you teach me wisdom in the inmost place" (51:6 NIV).

It's important that you stay open and honest with God during this process toward genuine forgiveness. Read through the psalms. They are brutally honest outcries to God, sometimes filled with anger and questioning. Engage God in that kind of honest dialogue. If you're not yet ready to forgive, tell it to God. He already knows, of course, but he can't heal you until you're honest about what you're feeling.

Obstacles to True Forgiveness

Those among us who simply excuse our husbands' behavior generally respond in one of two ways. One is, "Oh, poor me; I'll just put up with the bum." The other is to quickly forgive and move on in an unhealthy codependency.

The "poor me" wife tells herself she is excusing her husband's sexual betrayal, but her words are coated with sarcasm and resentment. She says things like, "All men are alike—they're just a bunch of philandering bums. Nothing he could do would surprise me!" Saying such things can be a part of processing anger, but when it becomes our only response, we're stuck in denial and pretending to forgive, while in reality we're carrying bitterness and resentment.

The codependent wife, a woman who is usually busy making sure everyone around her is okay, is accustomed to denying her own feelings. Rather than confront her husband, she'll usually make excuses for his hurtful actions. One friend told me that if her husband ever had an affair, she'd blame herself because it would mean she wasn't making him happy. But to be passive, to play possum and pretend your marriage isn't in deep trouble, is to refuse to participate with the realities under your own roof. We must actively confront the betrayal if we want to heal our marriage, grow as an individual, and work toward a mutually satisfying and truly intimate marriage relationship. Ignoring the betrayal or pretending it never happened leaves you trapped in an unfulfilling marriage.

Both these responses let us play a victim role while striking a pose of spirituality and selflessness. When we see ourselves as victims, we're frozen in powerlessness and helplessness—unable to think, feel, and act like a mature woman who can deal with what's going on in her marriage. But we're not victims, even though we may have been victimized. Author, therapist, and poet Juanita Ryan says:

> What we are saying about ourselves when we consider stepping into the fullness of healing and forgiveness, is that no matter what has been done to us, even though our offender treated us as if we were not lovable or valuable, the truth is we

are loved and valued. We are saying that even though we have been victimized, these events do not tell us *who we are.* We acknowledge that no matter how badly we were treated, we are and always have been, and always will be, beloved children of God.[11]

What Forgiveness Requires

As I've talked to dozens of women and heard their painful stories, many have modeled the forgiveness process for me. We can learn from these beautiful examples of God's love and grace, but we can also learn from the wisdom that enabled them to deal appropriately with their husbands' behavior.

Honesty with Ourselves

A friend told me about a woman named Eileen whose husband's rampant sexual addiction lasted for the first thirty years of their marriage. I couldn't imagine living through thirty long years filled with pornography, affairs, and prostitutes. I wanted to meet her and hear more of her story, so I called her and set up a luncheon date the following week at a little Italian restaurant. Several days later, sitting across from her in a bright red booth with garlic wafting through the air and Dean Martin singing "That's Amore" in the background, I heard Eileen pour out an amazing story of God's grace.

I was most awestruck, I think, by her staying power. I asked how she could possibly forgive her husband and rebuild her marriage after so many horrible years filled with incredible pain and loneliness. She told me how hard the years had been, how she finally confronted him and moved out, and how eventually God honored her efforts. After all those years, her husband took the steps necessary to turn his life around. It was during this period that Eileen learned deep lessons about forgiveness.

Forgiveness toward my husband became a possibility after confronting my own broken character. I recognized that we all sin, that in God's eyes my husband's sexual sins weren't any dirtier than my ongoing anger. We all have to take our guilt to the foot of the cross. My view of the cross changed during that process. You know, the ground is level at the foot of the cross. Without the cross, we're all lost. Not just those with sexual addictions—all of us.

Denise, whose story we've heard in earlier chapters, is open and honest about the reality that complete forgiveness may take time. I appreciated her honesty as she shared her forgiveness process with me.

I have to be honest and say that that's something I'm still working on. But what I can say so far in my process is that I don't think I would be able to forgive at all if I hadn't become aware of my own sins and mistakes. That's a huge thing, because for a long, long time, I thought it was just him wronging me, that I didn't do anything wrong in the marriage, that I was the victim.

One of the amends Eric made to me was to tell me that, "Until the last year or two, I hadn't seen you as a person. I saw you as a sexual object that I could manipulate to get my next fix." He said I was either in the way, or going along with meeting his need. When he made amends for that attitude toward me, I was able to forgive because I've become aware that I have hurt him, too—not in the same way, but in other ways.

Eileen and Denise have demonstrated the grace behind the saying, "No one can forgive another except he be aware of his own need to be forgiven." Becoming aware requires honesty with ourselves—honesty about our own failures and brokenness.

Separating the Wrongdoer from the Wrong

Lewis Smedes speaks eloquently about this necessary aspect of forgiveness.

> When you forgive someone for hurting you, you perform spiritual surgery inside your soul; you cut away the wrong that was done to you so that you can see your "enemy" through the magic eyes that can heal your soul. Detach that person from the hurt and let it go, the way a child opens his hands and lets a trapped butterfly go free.[12]

Earlier we heard about Tina and her pastor husband who had an affair. Tina became able to separate the wrong, the adultery, from the wrongdoers, her husband and the other woman, when she found the grace to work through her feelings. Tina said:

> They were both very needy people, and people who are needy do some really foolish things. And she was a very needy person. It doesn't make it okay, but I know she was miserable in her marriage and she was just crying out for help, and she cried out to her pastor and it led to more.

Tina's grace amazes me. But she reached this place of honest forgiveness by doing a lot of hard work. For most of us, grace this encompassing doesn't come easily.

Repeating Forgiveness

What does it mean if some of our hurt and resentment returns? Does it mean we didn't really forgive? I don't think so. I believe that Dr. Alan Loy McGinnis answers this question with wisdom and insight, and his words take care of our concerns about forgiving "perfectly." He says:

> Since all of our relationships vacillate, and since our internal emotions also have great variation, it is indeed quite likely that their resentment will return. Does this mean that the experience of forgiveness was invalid? Not at all. When Jesus said we were to forgive 70 times 7 times, I suspect that he had precisely such relationships in mind. They are not laid to rest with one act. We will find ourselves forgiving again and again, in the same manner that God forgives us.[13]

I certainly experience those vacillations in my own life. At times when my self-esteem is fragile, I can get hooked when I let myself wonder how Pat is doing with the sexual temptations all around him. When I do that, my mind goes back to old hurts and then the old anger and fear rush in. When I let myself fall prey to revisiting old wounds, I have to go back to the basics, exercise seventy-times-seven forgiveness, and plead with God to help me.

Honesty about the Price of Any Reunion

Reunion requires a price be paid. Smedes talks about this price in clear terms when he says, "I may forgive you in my heart and free myself from my hatred of you, but before I rejoin you as my friend, I demand a price from you. The price is honesty. The currency of honesty is remorse and conversion. And there is no reunion unless the price is paid."[14]

The Bible backs us up on this. The apostle Paul was very clear in his letter to the Christians in Ephesus. And *The Message* pulls no punches in this passage—honesty is the ticket to reconnection. Listen to Paul's words in Ephesians 4:25 spoken in today's language:

> And I insist—and God backs me up on this—that there be no going along with the crowd, the empty-headed, mindless

crowd. They've refused for so long to deal with God that they've lost touch not only with God but with reality itself. They can't think straight anymore. Feeling no pain, they let themselves go in sexual obsession, addicted to every sort of perversion. . . .

What this adds up to, then, is this: no more lies, no more pretense. Tell your neighbor the truth. In Christ's body we're all connected to each other, after all. When you lie to others, you end up lying to yourself.

No more lies. No more pretense. God understood human nature when he inspired that passage. Sandy Wilson tells how her husband finally told his story with honesty. In so doing, he paid the price required for forgiveness and reconciliation:

> To nurture my ongoing trust, Earl has to be willing to share. Part of it's just listening, part of it's asking questions. This is one of the areas we've grown in. When I bring something up, instead of saying, "No, I'm not," he'll say, "Tell me some more, talk to me some more about what you've observed," or something similar. That has really helped us, because I don't feel like he's going to become defensive so we're able to share. When he comes to me and shares something that he's struggling with, or a temptation he's experiencing, I can help him brainstorm about what's the best thing to do. Sometimes if I'm feeling too vulnerable and it's something that's hard for me to hear, I'll ask him to share with someone else. He'll go to another male friend and that's been helpful.

Sandy demonstrates maturity that seems beyond our human ability. Her emotional and spiritual health point toward our goal. In order to live with our husbands' secret wars, we need to become a safe person for them, a partner they can come to when they struggle. When there's that kind of honesty between husband and wife, marriage not only fulfills our longing for the deepest kind of intimacy, it propels our own spiritual growth.

Denise, whose husband Eric was addicted to pornography, shares how Eric's honesty sets the stage for forgiveness. But their story also portrays the hard, consistent work the husband—and the wife—must do.

> Mostly I'm able to forgive because there's something about when he comes to me and talks about how things really were that my heart is softened toward him. I don't know how I would respond if he wasn't working hard in his recovery program; I don't think forgiveness would be appropriate if he wasn't doing his work. But when he comes to me with his heart in the right place and sees me as a person, it's almost like the forgiveness just comes with it.
>
> I can sense when he's in a "shaky" place in his abstinence from pornography. It still creates in me that feeling of wanting to be the only one he has eyes for. I think as wives we have the right to be the only one. Yet I also need to recognize that he's human and he has a problem. I will let him work on that problem, but I also have feelings that go along with it. When I've seen a real genuine remorse on his part, it makes the forgiveness a whole lot easier. If he wasn't working on his recovery, I couldn't forgive while still living in the situation.

Denise's words communicate a measure of trust when Eric opens his heart with honesty. Does that mean that trust is a requirement of forgiveness? No. No authority nor Scripture that I've encountered names trust as a requirement for forgiveness. But trust is a wonderful goal.

157

Trust

Trust requires time—time for a husband to change and grow. Trust requires a track record, a pattern of consistent ongoing trustworthiness. Trust requires empathy from the husband. He needs to acknowledge the hurt and pain his actions have caused you. And trust requires grief. He must feel genuine remorse for the losses his sin created. David Augsburger's words express it strongly. He says, "forgiveness does not mean returning to business as usual but crafting a new relationship with a level of intimacy appropriate to our level of trust . . ."[15]

I asked several women I've counseled or who we've interviewed on our show about their renewal of trust. Pam Crist had this to say:

> Trust? I knew I couldn't trust him. When I agreed to move up here with him and start rebuilding our marriage and family again, it wasn't because I could trust him. But I knew where our hearts were that night, and I knew there was One I could trust who would never let me down. So the trusting didn't begin with trusting him, but with trusting God and trusting that he could help me get healthy.

Pam's husband, Richard, shared what he did to begin earning her trust, and about that process in their marriage.

> I came completely clean with my wife. I went through all the details, and I just laid it all out there. I had to come completely clean, and I encourage the men I work with to come clean as well, because if there's even one secret left, you've left one secret to build on and you won't heal—you won't recover—until you come completely clean.

Pam told how hard this was for her:

It's difficult to hear all that stuff. It's not easy, and I wouldn't encourage any man to do it without having a counselor present to help and to support his wife. It can be very hurtful. But Rich did a lot of other things, too, to help rebuild my trust. He was careful about what he watched on TV, he didn't go to places like 7–11 stores where there was pornographic temptation, and he started changing his thought patterns.

And Eric's willingness to listen to Denise has played an important part in building trust in their marriage, too. Denise shares honestly about where she is in that process:

I'm there! My mind works in numbers. When his abstinence from pornography is shaky, it's harder, but we've come a long way with that. The main difference is that Eric listens to me now when I point out sexual concerns—that has helped build trust. Trust has a price. Someone has to earn your trust, especially when there's a sexual addiction. I've lived too many years with a sex addict. I know the cycles of remorse, and feeling bad, and wanting to get help. Since I finally took my stand, none of that has washed for me. He had to get help. There had to be consistency. There had to be a willingness to work. There had to be a track record of abstinence. The trust has grown out of all that. For the first several months, I just sat back and observed, but as more time has gone on, a lot more trust has developed.

If we're in bed and I feel like I'm being used as a sex object—like it used to be all the time—I now respect my body more. When I feel used, I let him know. Last time this happened, I started crying and told him what I was feeling. He wasn't aware that he was feeling those feelings, but a few days later, he realized he was starting to slip and give in to temptation;

159

it had just taken him longer to become aware of it
than it had taken me.

Lewis Smedes agrees with Denise's position, and he
expresses it with firmness:

> They [the offender] cannot give you truthfulness in their
> words alone. . . . their honesty must be born in listening. The
> price of their ticket into your life is an open ear; an open mouth
> gets them only half way. They must listen to you until they
> hear your claims and your complaints and your cries.[16]

Right now you may feel like you'll never be able to trust
again. But trust is possible, if you know the long, hard steps
you have to take, and your husband is willing to trudge up
those steps with you. The process requires perseverance and
patience from both of you.

Honesty about Future Possibilities

If we want the chance to reconcile with our husbands,
we must bravely open the door to our hearts and invite them
back in. If they refuse to pay the price required for reunion—
honesty, remorse, accountability, and spiritual growth—we
can only open our hands and release them to God. But the
future always carries possibilities for new beginnings. When
we forgive, we create the opportunity for a happier future,
whether or not our husbands join us in that journey. Eileen's
story reflects the hope the future always carries if we do our
part in the healing process.

> Sexual addiction brings a lot of pain to a marriage,
> and grieving thirty years of that pain has been a
> process. There are still times when I grieve the
> heartache and losses, even though I can say I'm glad
> I hung in there with my marriage. I feel like we've only
> been married for two years, because it's only been in

the last two years that it has become a real marriage. Now we enjoy each other's company, and we begin our day by praying together. I can't say that all the heartache was worth it, or that I wouldn't change what we've been through if I could, but I can say I'm glad I hung on.

And Sandy Wilson encourages us to take the difficult steps required to grieve, forgive, and heal so that beyond this work, we can encounter a new beginning. For her, the new beginning included her husband.

I don't want to tell people that it's easy to put your marriage back together. It is not easy. In fact there have been times when I said, "Divorce couldn't be as hard as this," but it has been so worthwhile. The relationship Earl and I have now is so much more than I ever dreamed our marriage relationship would be.

I really encourage anybody who is considering this step [of confronting] to take it. Get some people who love the Lord to come around you and pray and confront and carry the two of you through the time. It's made such a wonderful difference in our marriage. I would not have chosen to live the way we were living before. I can honestly say I like the way we are now.

And Pam shares the hope and the future God had for her and Richard:

I gave Richard to God, and God was able to do something that I couldn't do in twenty-three years. He made a beautiful man out of him. I don't know of a man who is more tender and humble, and I just thank God for every moment we have together. When I work with women, I encourage them to focus on the One whom they can trust. And the forgiveness is also

161

for you because holding that bitterness will eat you alive, and you will become sicker than he is. And so we work on ourselves, because that's all we can do.

There Are No Guarantees

The agonizing, gut-wrenching truth about forgiveness is that there are no guarantees. No matter how hard we pray or how hard we work, we can't be certain he will never again give in to sexual temptation and betray his commitment.

Earlier we heard the story of the Christian actors, Carol Anderson and Jim Shores. Jim worked hard to leave the homosexual lifestyle behind. I asked Carol what it was like for her when Jim fell into old behavior and had a homosexual encounter during the first year they were married. Carol said:

> It was difficult. He told me what had happened and I was kind of in shock. I told him I forgave him, which to my ability at that time, I really did mean. But it took months with God's help for me to really, down to the depths of my soul, forgive. I had to go through my pain, I had to talk to friends, and I talked to my Christian counselor, and she helped me grieve and wrestle through it. And Jim and I talked a lot. He began working with a counselor again, too.
>
> I guess the biggest thing—the same as if it had happened in a heterosexual manner, was that we had to build trust again. I'd sometimes be scared that a conflict would propel him to go and seek someone out. I had to learn to trust him and to believe that he was working on his stuff. It wasn't like it happened and he just said, "Gee, I'm sorry," and didn't do anything else about addressing what had prompted this behavior. He was working on it, and I had to come to a place where I could let go. I had to trust that he wasn't

repeating the behavior but that he was being true to what he said.

I think it took about six months before I would quit holding my breath when he left the house. I wanted to interrogate him about where he went and who he saw. And then slowly we started getting back our comfort with each other, and to laugh together again, and things got a lot better.

Carol and Jim's story reflects the painful reality: There *are* no guarantees. But if we ever want the chance to reconnect with our husbands, we must take the risk required.

This process is slow. For some it may take years. But forgiveness—when we finally arrive at its door, not yet knowing if we have the courage and strength to open it, much less to walk through it—is in reality something we do for ourselves, not for the one who hurt us. Realizing the door opens into a room free from the bondage of his actions strengthens our grasp on its handle, and supplies the energy needed to shove it open, and to pass through it, however slowly.

If forgiveness eludes you and you feel stuck in your pain and anger, I encourage you to return to the grieving process. As Jack McGinnis said earlier in this chapter, forgiveness comes as a gift when we've completed healthy grieving. I encourage you to trade in your pillow full of thorns for one filled with rose petals so you can rest in the peace found in grace. And when you finally arrive at grace, there is no better way to nourish it than to reach out to others whose pain is fresh on the heels of their husbands' betrayal. You will find the strength and encouragement you need by sharing with others what you have learned.

-10-

Finding the Courage to Begin Again

Moving through the Muddle

> "Who are you?" said the Caterpillar.
> "I—I hardly know, Sir, just at present,"
> Alice replied rather shyly, "at least I know who I was
> when I got up this morning, but I think I must have
> been changed several times since then."
>
> *Lewis Carroll,*
> *Alice's Adventures in Wonderland*

Most women feel like Alice, lost in a foreign place, when they first discover their husbands' sexual betrayal. One minute they are a wife, possibly a mother, with a secure home life and a husband to help. Then in that moment when they discover the sexual betrayal, their identity changes, and they wonder, "Where am I and what do I do now?"

One young mother named Cynthia called in during one of our broadcasts. Her life had changed completely, and she knew she had to somehow begin again, yet she felt uncertain and lost. A heavy sadness hung over her words as she quietly told her story.

> My husband had an affair with his secretary, and he married her right away—right after the divorce. He left when we had a brand-new baby, so I've been feeling extreme pain as I watch our baby grow, knowing her father didn't care enough to be a part of his family. I've also been left basically destitute. That's been awfully hard, too. It's been a year and a half now and I still ache. It's very hard to see him with the kids when he picks them up for his visits. Knowing he's married and there's no way for us to be together ever again—that's the hardest part to deal with.
>
> I've been fortunate, though. Friends have just come out of the woodwork, especially because I had a brand-new baby. And I've formed a really close relationship with God, which has saved my sanity. But I've reached a place where I know I've got to move ahead because I'm not healing. I think that moving away to start over again with the kids, away from seeing my husband and the woman together, is the only way it's going to get better. That's where I'm headed, because it's very painful to run into them all the time. I don't know of any other solution. That means, of course, making new friends and losing my old ones and losing all the support they give me. But if I stay here, it's like continually pouring salt in my wound. I hope moving will help.

Cynthia is wandering through the mixed-up, muddled land called transition, the time between what was in the past and what will be in the future. Right now she lives in neither world and has no map to guide her on her journey. William Bridges, author of *Transitions: Making Sense of*

Life's Changes, explains the confused identity Cynthia is experiencing:

> Who we think we are is partly defined by the roles and relationships we have, both those we like and those we do not. . . . Our whole way of being—the personal style that makes you recognizably "you" and me "me"—is developed within and adjusted to fit a given life pattern.[1]

Recognizing that who we are has changed—because our most important human relationship has changed—helps us understand why this transition is so painful. For some of us, like Cynthia, the change is far-reaching because our marriage ends in divorce. For others, our mate remains, but our relationship with him—and we, ourselves—*need* to change if we hope for a better tomorrow. Recognize that transitions create confusion. Something has ended and we flounder, feeling lost and distressed.

Sandy Wilson certainly felt that confusion. As I mentioned before, she says, "One day I wanted to run, and the next day I wanted to stay. I was really up and down for probably a full year."

Sandy's marriage survived, but if your marriage is one of those that doesn't make it, the transition is even more difficult.

If the Marriage Ends

Whether your marriage ends because your husband walked away or because you just couldn't go on living with him after you discovered his secrets, you will collide with your grief again and again during the transition period that separates the past from the future. The ache you feel will eventually ease, but for now, your pain may be almost unbearable.

Nothing you do will end your grief quickly. Losing a marriage is like cutting away a part of yourself. It's important, for the sake of long-term healing, that you allow yourself to fully grieve your loss. You do need support during this time, and divorce recovery groups offer friendship and a healing community where others understand exactly what you're going through.

Church-based recovery groups also provide a biblical framework to help you deal with misplaced guilt and shame over the divorce. They will also help you understand God's love and grace and remind you of his promises to give you a hope-filled future. If your church doesn't have such a group, call some of the other churches in your area. If there simply aren't any such groups in your town or city, perhaps you could start one with the help of your pastor or another mature Christian who has gone through a divorce. You could also check with your local Christian bookstore to find the latest Christian books on divorce recovery.

One woman called our show recently to share what she had gained from her church's divorce recovery program:

> When I first began attending, I was convinced that even though my husband divorced me because of his affair with another woman, I was doomed for the rest of my life to be out of God's will as a divorced person. The people there helped me see, from God's Word, that I was not some kind of second-class citizen. They helped me see that God was committed to me and my children and that he would ultimately create beauty out of ashes.

If There's Hope for the Marriage

If there is still hope for your marriage, your feelings will be different than those of women who lose their marriage. Your pain and confusion, however, may still be overwhelming. Everything will remind you that rainbows and promises and a certain kind of naive innocence evaporated before your eyes, and that only God can renew your relationship with your husband and save your marriage.

For the two of you to heal and build a new future, you need God and others to uphold you as individuals and as a couple during your rebuilding process. Even with support, complete healing may take years for both you and your husband. Sandy Wilson's husband, Earl, found that it took much longer than he thought it would. As Earl told us during our radio interview, "Day after day I had to recognize that true repentance isn't just saying you're sorry, it's turning and going the other way. It took me most of three years to reprogram my mind."

And that means his wife, Sandy, had to live with that three-year process—both his process and her own. Understanding the nature of transitions helps us set realistic expectations for the work ahead of us.

Going through Transitions

Transitions have a characteristic shape and recognizable stages. William Bridges explains:

> Every transition begins with an ending. We have to let go of the old thing before we can pick up the new—not just outwardly, but inwardly, where we keep our connections to the people and places that act as definitions of who we are.[2]

To begin our transition, then, we must let go of what was, releasing our husbands and our marriages to God. Only then can we begin our journey across the desert that separates our old life from a new one.

All the work outlined in the previous chapters provides the vehicle for this crossing. That work—finding support people, letting go of codependency, learning to confront, shoring up weakened self-esteem, facing our own character defects, making amends, grieving our losses, and beginning the forgiveness process—all that work takes place in the in-between time that separates what was in the past and what is to be in the future. As William Bridges says, "Things end, there is a time of fertile emptiness, and then things begin anew. And it is to that characteristic sequence that we must now turn."[3]

Facing the "Other Woman"

For Tina, a pastor's wife whose story we read earlier, part of that transition process was a need to face the "other woman" and confront her with what she had done to Tina and her family. This is how she describes that meeting:

> About four months after the affair came out, I actually met with this other woman (who was one of my best friends) with her counselor and my counselor—so there were four of us present. That was one of the greatest steps in my healing. Not so much for me to be able to say, "I forgive you," but I felt like I needed to be able to ask her some direct questions, hear her answer, then go away and process it. In my heart, as a Christian, I knew that whether or not I felt like it, I needed to forgive her as Jesus Christ has forgiven me. Meeting with her and talking with her put closure on our friendship. I was also able to share how I felt. Just expressing my anger toward her, and expressing the hurt she caused my children who played with her children—just expressing those feelings took so much weight off me.

Part of Tina's transition involved putting closure on her past friendship with the woman who'd had an affair with her husband. Facing her helped her let go of what was and helped her move forward on her way to what would be.

Staying Connected to God

We don't have to walk across our transition and into the future alone. God wants to walk with us. Corrie ten Boom used to say, "Never be afraid to trust an unknown future to a known God." If he could help Corrie survive the concentration camps, we can trust him to help us through the penitentiary of our present fear and pain. Trusting God requires faith, and "Faith," wrote Tagore, the Indian poet, "is the bird that feels the light and sings while the dawn is still dark."

Trusting God when we're frightened and full of pain requires that kind of faith—faith to sing while the dawn is still dark, before there is a hint of sunlight and hope. One hurting wife told me, "I need to have a strong enough relationship with God so that when life presses in like this, resting in his arms is a very familiar place. More than anything I've ever gone through in my life, this experience has shown me I need to strengthen my relationship with God."

Arranging Temporary Structures

When the man we've loved and leaned on suddenly isn't there, or when he is completely absorbed in dealing with his own failures, we must develop other support to help us through our transition. Tina finally found that support when she and her husband decided to leave the church where he had pastored and attend a different one. Tina shares the hope she felt that first Sunday they attended the new church:

> We went to a different church about eight months after my husband's affair. For the first time I heard that there was hope for the future, and I remember feeling so refreshed when we left the service. Now I'm involved in a support group with other women whose husbands have been unfaithful in a variety of ways.

This group has been so good for me. I grew up in a Christian home, and I was so naive. I felt like if I was sexually there for Dave, he wouldn't look anywhere else, but in my group I've learned that many, many Christian men fight battles with sexual issues. We have a lot of wrong ideas as Christians, especially as Christian women. We just have to be more open with each other.

Taking Care of Ourselves

During this transition time you will be easily hurt, easily angered, and easily depressed. Realize that comes with the territory; give yourself some grace. You may suddenly burst into tears during a romantic movie or during a friend's wedding, or for no reason at all. For a while, your pain bottle will be so full of your own pain that even little things that touch your heart may cause your bottle to overflow. Finding old mementos of your life with your husband can be especially painful. On the other hand, mementos filled with meaning about who you are as an individual will connect with happier memories and strengthen your ability to recognize the positive qualities God gave you.

Do you, like me, keep little treasures from special times and special people in your life? I still have boxes filled with memories I hold dear. One box contains a beautiful letter my mother wrote to me and my sister during the time she was so ill that we went to live with relatives in another state, cards from my grandparents who are no longer living, and some velvety red towels (I love red!) that my father gave me to compliment me for a job well done. Another box holds loving notes, memories, and artwork from my children as they grew up—treasures of my years as a mother. Yet another package filled with cards, love letters, and other keepsakes from Pat sits on my closet shelf. Each of these tells me that in spite of my flaws, I'm still loved and valued.

Sift through your own special memories and treasures when your grief presses in. Anything that tells you that you are a special, valuable person can help bolster your self-worth and provide a boost of emotional energy for the transition through which you're passing.

Another way to take care of yourself might be to journal. Although I don't journal on a regular basis, I do write down my feelings during life's toughest times. When we journal, we can spill out our thoughts—our anger, hurt, and questions to God. It's a way to get it all out rather than holding it in. With thoughts and feelings on paper, it's much easier to sort through them and get in touch with what's going on inside.

When our husbands' sexual behaviors have hurt us, our egos sag. Almost anything that makes us feel better about ourselves sounds appealing, and for most of us, the biggest ego boost comes from other men's attention since it's *our* man's attention we're not getting. But getting these emotional hits only blurs the work we need to do, and if we become involved with other men, we set back our recovery from our husbands' betrayal. Adeena told me how she started down that path:

> In an effort to boost my wilted self-worth, I began flirting and trying to get male attention and approval. The attention part worked. At one point, I was juggling dates with three different men at once, which felt deceitful. I wasn't ready for emotional involvement then; it only made me feel worse.

Adeena wisely decided to stop dating until she had had some time to focus on healing, and she turned her attention to working through her recovery process. Eventually she healed enough to begin establishing relationships with men for the right reasons rather than just to boost her flagging ego.

Finding Help in Helping Others

George Bernard Shaw once said that happiness is a perfume you can't pour on others without spilling some on yourself. This simple little insight carries a powerful truth; we can't help others without receiving something back—the love of a hospitalized child, the grateful heart of a senior citizen, or the knowledge you're making life a little easier for the people lined up at the local food bank.

There is one caution we need to observe: Helping others can be used to avoid doing our own healing and growing work. Balance is the key. Let God be your guide as you seek ways to deal with your pain without denying or repressing it.

Remembering God Isn't through with Us Yet

For some among us, God miraculously knits together our past and our future, as he did for the actors, Carol Anderson and her fiancé, Jim Shores. Carol tells how God eventually led them back together after Jim broke off their engagement:

> I moved to North Carolina so I could attend UNC Chapel Hill and get my master of fine arts degree in acting. Jim, I thought, was spending another year in Houston, Texas. He didn't know where I was or how to get in touch with me. I needed some time to heal, so I hadn't let him know what was going on in my life.
>
> When it came time to register for my classes, I chose the final hour of the school's eleven-hour registration process. I was standing in the registration line in the A's, since my last name starts with A. The girl behind the table said to me, "Go over there to the cashier, right past the S's," so I did. And as I turned to my right, there stood Jim in the line. I couldn't believe he was there! He didn't see me, so being a woman, the first thing I did was put on my makeup; and then I started shaking.

173

Miraculously, God began to bring us back together, but for a while I felt like I was doing all the giving. I was still in love with him, but Jim was still working hard on his homosexual lifestyle issues. For a while, graduate school and dealing with his sexual issues took so much of his energy that he didn't have any time left for me. I was kind of frustrated, because with my counselor's help, I had done so much work to grow and heal, yet my relationship with Jim was still difficult. I couldn't figure out what God was doing.

I finally said to God, "It's okay if he's out of my life and if we never get married. It's okay; I do not need him to be a whole person." I really let go of Jim. It was soon after that time that Jim moved into a place in his healing where he could actually reach out again, and we re-fell in love! All the best things I loved in him from the start were still there, but there was also a richness and a strength that had not been there before, and a year later we were married.

Carol's story ended with a beautiful wedding, but for some, the past is cut from the future by a channel flowing with a new way of life. Margaret's story is proof that even though we may lose our husbands, God is faithful, and if we follow his leading and do the tough work required to move through our loss, he will lead us into a new life. During a phone call, Margaret shared how God began weaving a new future into the tapestry of her life:

God has been working powerfully in my life since my husband left me and our sons. That first year I discovered a wonderful church through an old friend who happened to call after my husband left. God has been using my new church family and my experiences there to love me and help me grow, along with a skillful therapist who helped me survive the divorce process.

Each step of the way, God takes me to deeper levels of my fears and pain, helps me face them and cleans out the wounds. He gifted me with the most wonderful accountability partner who's been there to support and love me and let me be me. God gave me a support group where I get the nurturing and support I didn't get from my husband or even from my own family. The group provided a safe place where I could take off my mask and cry out my pain. He provided godly men in my life so I could learn all men are not jerks and that you can get safe hugs in a safe place with people who love you just because you're you.

As a friend always asks me when I start to get discouraged, "Margaret Ann, how big is your God?" He's big enough to free me from my fears of my ex-husband, to help me deal with the past, and to trust his light to shine on the truth. He knew the change in my life was coming. He prepared me for it, and he's providing his abundance during it.

During a difficult time in my life, a wise friend told me, "Life is teaching you some painful lessons. But it is from adversity that strength is born. You may have lost the inning, but I know you'll win the game." This promise may sound hollow right now, but with God's help and loving support, you *will* win the game, like so many women who've walked the path before you.

Explore New Opportunities

When our husbands break our trust, something freezes inside, and we go into a kind of emotional shock. As God begins to thaw that frozen place, we are freed to reach out for a new life. As you discover you *are* still alive, open your life to new opportunities and set new goals, whether you are alone or your husband remains with you. Life has changed, and you *are* growing even though it is terribly painful. As Margaret thawed and discovered she was still alive, God gave her new opportunities and a whole new life.

> I feel like I've been on God's fast track ever since my husband left and I rededicated my life to the Lord. I am now a support group leader at my church. I began and graduated from a master's program in counseling psychology, and I am now a marriage and family counselor helping others. Life hasn't been perfect—it's been a long and difficult process of personal and family recovery.
>
> I've been pushed out from behind the safety of my walls to proclaim my hope—my God is a God of impossible situations, and I do expect a miracle. As Romans 5:3–5 says, "we also rejoice in our sufferings, because we know that suffering produces perseverance; perseverance, character; and character, hope. And hope does not disappoint us, because God has poured out his love into our hearts by the Holy Spirit, whom he has given us" (NIV).

Like Margaret, you, too, have choices. How would you like the next chapter of your life to read? Is there some goal you have put off for years? Life is filled with choices; I love Juanita's poem "Choices." It captures the freedom and the terror contained in taking responsibility for crafting a new future.

Choices

Will I scurry away
like a frightened little creature,
fleeing, hiding, trapped?
Or will I beat powerful wings
to high away places,
gliding, soaring,
free?

One of my favorite inspirational sayings is taped on my desk where I can see it every day: "And the day came when the risk to remain tight in a bud was more painful than the risk it took to blossom." I read this whenever I feel afraid to try something new—whenever I'm tempted to remain closed and safe like a rosebud. But when my need for growth feels so strong that it hurts, I know I have to take the risk that growth and change require—I have to open up and blossom. Remember this rosebud image when change feels scary. If it's time for growth in your life, risk opening yourself to new opportunities and experiences.

Out of Death Comes Life

Tina knows about death and rebirth. Although she and her pastor husband salvaged their marriage, something did die. But, thank God, death doesn't have to be the end of the story for God's children. I asked Tina what her message would be to other women whose husbands have committed sexual sin. She was silent for a moment and then said:

> I would say that out of death comes life, and there is hope. You don't have to look at crisis as an ending point for your marriage; it can be a beginning. That is true in our situation. I'm thankful that God saved our marriage and that now we can help other people going through something similar. It's been painful and hard, but we have a new life. It's been a difficult experience for our kids as well, but now they have a true sense of what forgiveness is, what repentance is. Our hope is that we can break the pattern of hiding our sin by becoming more open and living a healthy new life as a family, committed more deeply than ever to love and to honesty.

Denise, who lived with her husband's sixteen-year-long addiction to pornography, has found a wonderful new relationship with her husband, Eric, as well. She shared this beautiful part of their story on our radio program:

> A couple of months after Eric began attending a Twelve Step group for pornography addiction and taking responsibility for his behavior, I was sitting out on the porch one morning eating breakfast. Eric came out of the house holding a book and asked me if I'd be willing to read a brief account of another sex addict's wife. He wanted to know what I felt about what she wrote.
>
> So I began to read. I felt like I was reading my own story. It was incredibly validating for me to know that I wasn't the only one who had lived with so much pain. Tears started streaming down my face. I remember we were sitting there and the sun was warm on our faces, and for the first time I felt like my husband really wanted to know what was in my heart and what all those years had really been like for me. It was so special, because I saw no defensiveness in his eyes. He was just sitting there, beside me, wanting to connect and wanting honesty from me. It's probably one of the purest moments that I have known in our nineteen years of marriage, going from that closed secrecy to opening up; it was like the sunshine on our faces— a beautiful moment. He really had my heart in the palm of his hand.

There is life beyond the dark valley you may be in. There is hope for a happy future for any of us if we choose to lean on our heavenly Father and on our support people and take the important steps toward growth and healing. Juanita's poem "The Wind" describes the unfreezing that takes place during healing in such a way that you can almost feel it. My prayer for you is that you, too, will once again "feel alive."

The Wind

For a very long time
I tried to hold still.
I contained my self.
Frozen-stiff. Unmoving.

Then one day a warm wind
spun itself around me
defrosting me
throwing me off balance.

I was moving.
Stumbling, turning.
And with each changing motion
came new freedom and surprise.

I am no stone statue.
I am alive!

11

Being There for Others

"Jesus with Skin On"

> He [God] comes alongside us when we go through
> hard times, and before you know it, he brings us
> alongside someone else who is going through hard
> times so that we can be there for that person just as
> God was there for us.
>
> *2 Corinthians 1:4,*
> *The Message*

One Friday evening a few months ago, we were at the radio station here in Seattle, ready to go on the air with our *Love Under Fire* broadcast like we do every week. That particular evening was the interview with Richard and Pam Crist, whom we've referred to earlier. As you've read, the Crists' marriage has been through some of the worst this world has to offer, yet has emerged with a powerful testimony of God's grace. There in our soundproof studio, sitting across the curved laminate counter sat Rich and Pam, earphones on and ready to tell their story to anyone who was listening, praying that God would use it to help keep other couples from making the mistakes they did.

Rich and Pam look like anyone else in their fifties: Time is beginning to draw lines on their faces, and Rich's hair is tinged with gray. Obviously in love, their smiles radiate peace and joy. From looking at them, you would never believe that rampant sexual abuse had once ruled their entire lives—pornography and extramarital affairs nearly destroyed them and their children. Now a kind and gentle man, Rich's eyes fill with tears when he tells how he physically abused Pam in the early years of their marriage.

As they told their story to the radio audience, Rich and Pam vulnerably shared about the sexual sin and substance abuse that characterized both of their lives for years, and about the healing they ultimately found as they rededicated their lives to God. The Crists are another one of God's miracles, proof that he can change lives. Having been through so much and then saved by God's grace, they now dedicate their lives to helping other people who are caught in the web of sexual addiction and the pain it inflicts on both the addicts and their families.

Several months after the broadcast, I picked up the phone and called Pam. I wanted to know how helping other women has helped her in her own efforts to grow and to not fall back into the patterns that used to run her life. Her response underlined the necessity of reaching out to others in need as a way of continuing to recover and grow ourselves.

> More than anything, having women come to me for help has driven me to my knees. It's forced me to have closer communication and a closer walk with God. It's caused me to not forget where I was. When I see their pain, I realize I have been there and don't ever want to be there again. I realize again that the only hope for any of us is at the feet of Jesus. In finding answers for these women, I find answers for myself, and I thank God again for the peace and joy he's

brought into my life as I've focused on taking the necessary steps to grow.

Before we can be encouragers to others, we have to have been faithful in our own walk. Through us, these women need to see that life will get better—that they won't always hurt as much as they do right now. When other women who are hurting see that God is helping me, they find hope that he will help them, too.

Pam is right. When you share your story with someone who is where you were, that person can find hope and courage to follow your steps to healing. Helping a woman who is in pain because her husband is involved with some form of inappropriate sexual behavior also helps us. This is so true in my life. Each time another hurting woman calls me, I am reminded that I, too, must keep my eyes off my husband and focus on my relationship with God and my own growth.

Sharing with Others

As I've said so many times in these pages, the energy and power to make successful change depends, in large part, on getting support. But another life principle is at work for Pam and me and all the others who are trying to encourage hurting women: If we want to sustain that change, there is no better way than to give to others the same encouragement and support we've received. By reaching out and sharing with others what we have learned, we make a commitment to them, but we also keep our own healing alive. It's so easy to fall back into wondering and worrying about what our husbands are thinking, feeling, or doing. The best insurance we can get comes from helping others. When we do, we realize just how much we've grown, and we are reminded of our own need to keep moving forward.

In his little book *Making the Break,* David Parington tells us that "We are called to be the reality of Jesus to others. To be his smile to those who are sad. To be his graciousness and gentleness to those who are hurting."[1] Or as author Keith Miller says, we're called to be "Jesus with skin on."[2] As humans, we need a human touch, one that represents Jesus' love. There is no greater privilege than to play that role in another person's life.

Earlier this year I led a seminar for a group of women in another part of the country. I did nothing special; I merely helped create a safe place where women could be honest about their hurts and find encouragement from one another. A few days after I returned home, I received this note from one of the women:

> Jesus with skin on—that's what you were to me and the other women while we shared each other's joys, pain, and sorrows. I truly felt like you cared about me. Now I just have to care about myself.

My heart was touched, and *I* felt cared about and encouraged! When we give from our hearts and experiences, God can use our simple message to help others, and we are helped as well. As we give and grow, we move farther and farther away from the old patterns of checking up on our husbands and worrying and wondering what they are thinking or doing.

The Gentle Art of Listening

Becoming an encouraging support for other hurting women doesn't require anything but a loving heart, a willingness to be transparent in sharing your story and the lessons you have learned, and a gentle ear for listening. Many times when a woman comes to me, she just wants someone safe to tell her story to, someone to cry with, and someone to pray with. And, oh so often, she asks me where she can get help from other women.

As you heal, ask God if he needs you to become "Jesus with skin on" for women who are where you were. It isn't hard. I've included a few simple guidelines that will help you be a "safe" person for other hurting women.

- Make it safe for her to share heart to heart. Leave all judgment at the door.
- Let her talk without interrupting her.
- Be careful when you share from your own experience; it's easy to take over without meaning to. This time is about *her* and her story.
- Remember that it's not your job to try to "fix" her.
- Use active listening skills like those below. She'll know you really care.
- Be aware of your own nonverbal body language; leave your arms uncrossed and your body "open" to "receive" her sharing. This openness helps her know you are a safe person to open up to.
- Be attentive; stay "with" the other person—track what she's saying as you listen.
- Encourage her and let her know you're listening by nodding your head, saying, "Mmm," and "Hmm, hmm," when appropriate.
- When she finishes sharing, gently ask a question, rephrasing what she said to see if you have heard and understood her correctly.
- Use gentle, open-ended questions to help her explore her feelings.
- Be comfortable with silence if she stops to think or cry. Don't try to hush her crying or shorten it. Those tears play an important role in the healing process.
- Don't jump in when she's finished to tell her what she needs to do.

- As her mentor, share how you struggled to grow and reach a place of serenity with your situation. Let her know the steps and processes that have helped you deal with your husband's sexual issues.
- Never judge her.
- Above all, become her friend.
- Pray with her and for her.
- Don't try to be a counselor—leave that to the professionals.
- When she's ready to look at her own issues and the places she needs to grow, be her accountability person if she wants you to.
- A word of warning—if you find yourself becoming codependent or being pulled down in your own growth, be mature enough to realize that this woman probably needs to find someone else to help her on her journey toward healing.

I received the following note from one woman I met with several times. It illustrates how healing can result from creating an environment that feels safe and nonjudgmental:

> Just meeting with you and seeing your calm and gentle spirit with me paved the way to provide a "safe" environment for me to open up and share. Thank you for being so accepting and treating me with integrity and respect. I felt as if I should or would be ashamed, but I wasn't, because you showed me unconditional love. That made me feel safe.

Continuing Our Own Growth

To continue to grow and remain strong, we need to stay close to our heavenly Father and practice what we've learned. This simple formula clarifies how we can stay on track in our own growth:

Knowledge + Practice + Support + Sharing = Change

Use this list to stay focused on your own work and growth.

Remember, the only person you can change is yourself.
Maintain your sources of support.
Continue reprogramming your codependent behaviors—those actions that are either controlling or motivated by people-pleasing.
Confront when necessary.
Continue to build your self-worth, always remembering you are a precious child of God.
When you fail or hurt someone, take responsibility for your behavior.
Make amends.
Grieve your losses when they come; don't let unexpressed pain and feelings build inside you. Try to find someone to talk to about it.
Forgive others as God forgives you.

Sandy Wilson, a woman whose story appears often in this book, looks back on where she was and where she is now. She and her husband, Earl, worked hard over a period of years to build a new, healthy life. Know that if you take the same steps, one day you, too, will have a beautiful story to tell. Sandy shares her story with the prayer that her words will encourage you:

> As I drink in the beauty of this crisp fall day, I am awed that I feel so at peace and so thankful for my life. Seven years ago, when my world shattered through the revelations of my husband's unfaithfulness, no one could have convinced me that I would ever celebrate life again.[3]

My prayer for you is that *your* story will also have a beautiful ending.

Appendix 1

How to Start
a Support Group

Investigate Existing Groups

Before you make a firm decision to start your own group, find out what support groups might already be operating in your area. If you live in a larger city, your search will probably be more productive than if you live in a rural community, but in either case, the best place to start is with a call to the nearest crisis line. Ask if they know of any support groups in your area for spouses of people who struggle with sexual addiction. It's unlikely that they'll have one, so also ask about groups such as Al-Anon and grief and bereavement groups. In addition, local female counselors sometimes offer small, therapist-led groups for women dealing with a particular difficulty. The crisis line may know about these or may be able to give you the name of a counselor who deals with women's issues.

If you are able to find or start a group where your Christian faith is incorporated into the meetings, you will experience greater healing and deeper connection with the other women. I encourage you to also check with one or more of the national resources such as the American Family Association or The National Association for Christian Recovery listed in appendix 3 of this book. If one of the counselors who is listed there lives in your area, give her a call.

If you are unable to find a group that meets your needs and feels comfortable and safe, it's time to move ahead and start a group of your own. Many women sitting in church pews in your community are right where you are—confused, hurting, and feeling very alone in dealing with their husbands' sexual behavior. And perhaps like you, they feel afraid to reach out to anyone. Pastors often know which couples in their congregations are dealing with sexual issues and which wives would benefit from such a group. Talk to different pastors in your area, using an anonymous name if you choose; use the telephone if that makes you more comfortable than meeting them face-to-face. Let them know your need and purpose and ask if they know of women in their churches who are dealing with the same issues. Ask the pastors to give these women your name and phone number (again, an anonymous name if you choose) and to encourage the women to call you so that you can begin to support one another.

Another good way to find possible group members is to ask if you can put a small notice on the church bulletin board or in the adult Sunday school classes. Notices on bulletin boards in Laundromats and grocery stores may also produce potential members. By making your group open to non-churchgoers in this way, you can also represent Christ's love to these women.

It may take a while to get a few women together, but begin meeting regularly as soon as you find even one other woman. Even if there are only two of you, you will find love, support, and understanding by sharing together on at least a weekly basis.

What a Support Group Is and Isn't

A support group provides a setting in which we can talk through problems openly and honestly in a safe environment with women like ourselves. In such a group, sharing feelings and experiences is welcome, no matter how ugly those might be. Not only can we share, we also heal and grow.

In John Baker's excellent *Celebrate Recovery* curriculum for small groups, he lists what support groups *are* and *are not*. The lists below are adaptations of his.[1]

Things We Are	Things We Are Not
A safe place to share	A place for gossip
A refuge	Therapy
A place of belonging	A place to judge others
A place to care for others and be cared for	A place to rescue or be rescued by others
A place where respect is given to each member	A place for perfection
A place where confidentiality is kept	A place to judge others
A place to grow and become strong again	A quick fix
A place for healthy challenges and risks	A place to tell others what to do
A possible turning point in your life	

Where and When to Meet

If you feel safe meeting in a small classroom in your church, ask your pastor if one is available that you can use on the day and time you choose for your meetings. Hospitals will sometimes let support groups use a small conference room for meetings that take place at night. Be creative and persistent until you find what you need. Consider schools, public libraries, and other churches in town. Your group may need to pay a small monthly fee; ask about this when you make your first contact.

You and the others who attend the first meeting will decide when and how long you want your meetings to be. Most groups run for about one-and-a-half hours. You will probably have difficulty finding a time that will work for everyone; just do the best you can.

Group Facilitators

Your group will need one person to serve as facilitator, or perhaps two to be co-facilitators. A facilitator is not a group "leader," nor is she supposed to have all the answers to the situations that come up. A facilitator merely insures that a certain structure exists and that group guidelines are followed. She may delegate many of the tasks to others—such as being a liaison with the church or other facility where you meet, keeping track of offerings and materials, making coffee and tea, and reading the guidelines at the opening of the meetings.

Group Guidelines

Experience has shown that groups that follow certain guidelines in the way they conduct their meetings are more successful than those that don't. These guidelines are based on three important needs: the need for confidentiality, the need to work on ourselves in the group and not try to fix others, and the need to avoid "cross talk." Let's look at each of these in more depth.

Confidentiality and Anonymity

For people to feel free to share openly and deeply, there *must* be an agreement among all members to keep confidential both what is shared in the group and the identity of the others in the group. This includes the kind of gossip that is disguised as "prayer requests." Telling no one what goes on in the group means *no one*—including your spouse or your pastor. Without strict adherence to this, the group will never become a safe place and will soon fall apart. Sharing your pain in an unsafe environment is like being asked to skinny-dip in a public pool. Confidentiality cannot be overstressed.

Focusing on Ourselves

In Matthew 7:3, Jesus encourages us to look at the "plank" in our own eye rather than at the "speck" in the other person's. That means we come to the group to work on our own problems, not someone else's. We don't come to fix the others in the group, to analyze other's motives or behavior, to ask others questions, or to allow our sharing to be dominated by stories about what our spouse did. Focusing on others, such as our husbands, helps us avoid our own issues, and makes us observers rather than true participants; those are not the reasons for the group. Instead, we come to share our personal needs, feelings, ideas, and problems—in short, to work on ourselves.

Avoiding "Cross Talk"

"Cross talk" involves any of the following behaviors: interrupting people when they share, asking them questions, having a dialogue with one other member of the group about what she is sharing, or negatively commenting on or evaluating what someone else has said in the group. It's called cross talk, because in a support group we sit in a circle, and if we talk *to* someone in the circle during the sharing time, we are talking *across* the circle. During our sharing time, we listen with our hearts, eyes, and ears, but we don't cross talk. If we do, members are afraid they won't be able to finish sharing and that others are judging what they say.

Instead, we listen respectfully and attentively to what each one shares. We support them by giving them our full attention, by nodding or smiling, or by gently murmuring "Thanks, Mary" when they finish. We do not intervene when one of the members cries or experiences other distressing emotions. Oftentimes, when we "comfort" others prematurely, we cut short their opportunity to feel and express *all* their emotions in a safe environment. Two of the wisdoms that a small group experience imparts to its members are that tears are not bad and loving, sympathetic silence during tearful times communicates deep respect for the person and her feelings.

To Be Read at Each Meeting

The principles for successful small groups fit into four key group guidelines. These four guidelines, along with the Serenity Prayer, should be read at the beginning of every meeting.

1. Keep your sharing focused on your own thoughts and feelings. Please limit your sharing to five minutes to make sure there is time for everyone. We can lengthen sharing if our group is small.
2. We are here to support one another as we each seek God's direction for our lives and marriages. We are not here to "fix" one another.
3. Anonymity and confidentiality are requirements that absolutely must be met. Who attends this group and what is shared in the group stays in the group!
4. There will be no cross talk, please. Cross talk includes interrupting, asking questions, or any back-and-forth conversation while in the sharing circle.

"God, grant me the serenity to accept the things I cannot change, the courage to change the things I can, and the wisdom to know the difference. Amen."

Content for Small Group

In appendix 2, "Workbook for the Healing Journey," you'll find suggested questions and exercises to help you gain the most from each of the eleven chapters in this book. To use *Living with Your Husband's Secret Wars* as the core material for your support group, simply ask each woman to read one chapter per week prior to coming to the support group and complete the written exercises for that chapter in the workbook section.

At each meeting, the facilitator picks one or more questions from the chapter you read that week as the focus for the group's meeting. To begin the group, read the guidelines to remind members what they need to do. Then go around the circle and "get clear"—which simply means going around the circle and allowing everyone the opportunity to share whatever tensions or burdens they may be carrying into the group. This process will help them focus more effectively on the topic for the evening.

After you've gone around the circle once "getting clear," introduce the topic for the evening. This is the heart of the support group, a time when women can share their deep feelings about the questions in the workbook that have been chosen for that week's work. Go around the circle again, letting each member share her feelings and what she wrote as she answered the questions (if she wants to). Let the sharing process take place naturally; if no one else begins the sharing, start with yourself, and others will follow.

Timetable (Example Only)

7:00 P.M. Opening prayer and welcome.
    Introductions (first names only).
    Read the Serenity Prayer out loud together.
    Read the support group guidelines.
7:10 P.M. First round of sharing: getting clear.
7:40 P.M. Second round of sharing. Use the questions that were selected for the week's focus.
8:20 P.M. Wrap-up and prayer request/closing prayer.
8:30 P.M. Announce next week's assignment in the book.

Group closes, then women may visit informally if they want to.

Finances

Each week an offering should be taken to cover the cost of room rental, coffee and tea, and copies of materials.

Prior to the First Meeting

Contact all the women who have indicated interest in the group. Discuss the purpose of the group, its general format and confidentiality, the book you'll be using and its cost. Order enough copies of *Living with Your Husband's Secret Wars* so that each woman has one. Ideally, each woman should have the book a week before the first meeting, and you should have one or two extra copies for each meeting in case someone comes unexpectedly. Ask the women to read the introduction and chapter 1 prior to the first meeting. Secure a facility for the meeting and give directions to each woman. Make copies of the support group guidelines and the Serenity Prayer.

First Meeting

Double check with the contact person at your meeting facility to confirm that the room will be ready—unlocked, heat on, and so on. Arrive early and make coffee and prepare hot water for tea. Arrange chairs in a circle. Greet women as they arrive and hand out copies of the support group guidelines and the Serenity Prayer. Remember, you're not there as the "expert" or the person with all the answers but rather as another woman who is dealing with her own feelings and wants to use this process to bring healing in all of your lives.

When everyone is seated, briefly explain the purpose of the group, then begin the actual meeting, using the format on page 193. During the reading of the group guide-lines, put special emphasis on the need for confidentiality. Since this is the group's first meeting, you need to discuss whether you want an "open group"—one where new women can come at any time or a "closed group"—one where no one else can come until your time as a group has ended.

This is also the time to discuss the length of time you want to be a group. Do you want to continue as a group until you've worked through the workbook, ending the group when fin-ished? Or would you rather go through the book's material once, then begin again, knowing that each member is free to stay on, quit, or start another group if more than eight or ten women want a group? For group size, ten is about the max-imum number in order to have time for everyone to share at each meeting.

As you attend meetings with women who struggle with many of the same feelings and experiences you do, as you begin to say what you're feeling and you open your heart and share your deepest pain, as you endeavor to move through the work outlined in this book and grow, you will discover that you are changing. Not only will you become stronger and more able to deal with the pain that your husband's sexual struggles bring into your life, you will also change in other ways. You will become more "real." You won't enjoy wearing a mask all the time; you will become more assertive in a healthy way; you will recog-nize your mistakes and take responsibility for them and make amends.

In short, you will begin to see God heal you and deepen your relationship with him. Just trust him one day at a time and take the next step he tells you to. And remember his promises.

"For I know the plans that I have for you," declares the LORD, "plans for welfare and not for calamity to give you a future and a hope. Then you will call upon Me and come and pray to Me, and I will listen to you. And you will seek Me and find Me, when you search for Me with all your heart. And I will be found by you," declares the LORD.

Jeremiah 29:11–14 NASB

Appendix 2

Workbook for the Healing Journey

*Questions to Use in Personal Study
or in Preparation for a
Weekly Support Group Meeting*

Chapter 1

1. How does your husband's inappropriate sexual behavior make you feel about him? About yourself?
2. Do you feel angry? At whom? In what ways have you expressed your anger?
3. Did you have a "gut feeling" that something was going on in your marriage? What was your response to that gut feeling?
4. In what ways have you ignored, put up with, or spiritualized your husband's behavior? How does that make you feel about yourself?
5. Have you tried to get back at your husband? How?
6. Have you asked him to be tested for sexually transmitted diseases? How did he respond? Did you or are you remaining sexually abstinent until you know he is a safe sexual partner? What are your rights to protect yourself from disease?

7. In what ways are you powerless over your husband?
8. Are you ready to do the hard work required to face reality and, with God's help, build a healthy life whether or not your husband stays with you?
9. Are you ready to release your husband, step back, and *really* turn your life and marriage over to God and trust him with the outcome? Can you say the Serenity Prayer and really mean it? "God, grant me the serenity to accept the things I cannot change, the courage to change the things I can, and the wisdom to know the difference. Amen."

Chapter 2

1. Do you feel isolated, helpless, and alone? Describe those feelings.
2. Have you told anyone else about your husband's sexual behavior? If so, what was the person's response?
3. Do you hide your emotional pain behind a mask? How long have you worn your mask? What does it cover?
4. How do you feel when you contemplate honestly sharing your situation and feelings with a "safe" supportive group of women who are going through a similar situation, if they are willing to be honest, as well? What would it take for you to feel safe with these women?
5. You have a right to your feelings and you need time to work through them. But are you willing to commit to a process of working through them until God enables you to release them and replace them with peace?
6. A counselor and/or a support group are crucial too as you work through your feelings, make decisions, and grow. Are you willing to make a commitment to yourself to locate or put together one or the other, but preferably both? Use appendix 1 as a guide for finding or starting a support group.

Chapter 3

1. Do you, like me, have to repeatedly release your husband to God, because you realize you are once again obsessing on what he might be doing or thinking? What thoughts or feelings repeat themselves most often?
2. Do you recognize codependency in your desire to control your husband's behavior? In what ways have you been codependent? Do you try to hide or deny your husband's behavior from others or isolate yourself? Are you emotionally needy? Are you fiercely independent and determined not to need anyone? Where do you think your codependency comes from? How did it start in your life?
3. Reread C. S. Lewis's quote on page 59. What emotions does that quote bring up in you?
4. Do you think your obsessive thoughts about your husband inhibit your own growth and walk with God, as well as your peace? In what ways?

Chapter 4

1. Describe how you feel when you consider confronting your husband about his inappropriate sexual behavior.
2. Do you see yourself as a victim of your husband's behavior? In what ways? How do you feel when you think about the future of your marriage? Does "helpless" describe your feelings? In what ways are you helpless?
3. Do you agree with Dr. Mark Laaser's statement, "To ignore this behavior would be to become a party to their sin"? Why or why not?
4. Do you agree with Dr. James Dobson's statement, "A *passive* approach often leads to the dissolution of the relationship. *Genuine* love *demands* toughness in moments of crisis"? Why or why not?

5. Can you financially afford to confront your husband and risk losing his income? If not, what possible resources do you have with your community, church, family, friends, or your own abilities?

6. As love begins to deteriorate, the vulnerable party—in this case the wife—usually begins to panic. Characteristic responses include lashing out, begging, pleading, grabbing, hollering, or even throwing things at him. Or the reaction may be just the opposite, involving appeasement and passivity. Do any of these actions describe you? Which ones?

7. Are you ready for respect—his and your own? Dr. Dobson says respect "is the critical ingredient in human affairs," and that it is "generated by quiet dignity, self-confidence, and common courtesy." What emotions and feelings inhibit you from relaxing into a calm, firm, steadfast spirit that knows it is appropriate to expect your husband to remain emotionally, mentally, and physically faithful, and to confront him when he's not?

8. Who might be able to help you plan and execute a confrontation? If no one else comes to mind, an addictions counselor should be both willing and able.

Chapter 5

1. In what ways has your husband's mental, emotional, or physical betrayal affected your self-esteem?

2. Do you ever compare yourself to other women? How do you feel when you are with your husband and a younger, prettier, or more glamorous woman is present?

3. What's your gut reaction when sensuality is flaunted in front of your husband, such as on the beach, at the movies, or on TV?

4. We know that we are each unique and the work of the Master Craftsman, even though it's hard to remember that right now. In what ways did God make you a special, unique individual?

5. Do you have people in your life who affirm your worth and let you know you are valuable and lovable? Who are those people? If no one comes to mind, how might you cultivate affirming relationships? Can a support group meet this need?

6. Assertiveness is a skill that communicates two-way respect—respect for others *and* respect for ourselves. It also increases our self-esteem because it helps us remember that we have value and rights. How do you rate on an assertiveness scale? Do you need to strengthen or quiet your assertiveness? If you lack assertiveness, what steps are you taking to build it into your relationships with others?

7. Growing and blossoming as a unique individual helps move us beyond victimhood and greatly increases our self-esteem. As you finish this workbook, be asking God to show you how you can develop any gifts he has given you that aren't being exercised in your life right now.

Chapter 6

1. Are you willing to turn the spotlight on yourself and examine your own character flaws? What is your reaction to this idea?

2. When you stand in that bright light and examine yourself, what do you see?

3. Do any of the negative relationship patterns listed in chapter 6 belong to you? Which ones?

4. Have you been sexually available to your husband throughout your marriage? Why, or why not? How do you think he feels about your sexual availability?

5. Would your husband say you are a "cold wife"? Do you touch him, hug him freely, and let him know you love and appreciate him?

6. How do you treat your emotional pain? Do any of the behaviors listed in chapter 6 fit you? Which ones?

7. As food for thought and personal insight, take the Socially Acceptable Addictions test and the Dependency on Men's Approval test below. Do these tests reveal new information to you about your need to work on certain areas in your life?

8. Are you ready to take responsibility for your negative relationship styles and the unhealthy ways you treat your pain? What steps can you take to eliminate them? How can your support group help you with this growth?

Socially Acceptable Addictions

FOOD

1. Do you eat when you are depressed, anxious, or angry?
2. Do you feel comforted when you eat?
3. Do you find yourself thinking about your weight or food several times through a normal day?
4. Do you struggle with feelings of low self-esteem because of your weight or eating habits?

SPENDING

1. Have you intentionally gone shopping to lift your spirits or help deal with depression rather than because you really needed something?
2. Have you sometimes hidden your purchases or lied about them so your family wouldn't know you had been shopping?
3. Have you felt guilty, remorseful, or anxious after a shopping spree?
4. Have you used one line of credit to pay off another?

WORK

1. Does your family complain about the long hours you work?
2. Do you rarely have time to be involved in school or social activities with your family?
3. Do you find that you have to keep constantly busy on various projects at home, even in the evenings and on the weekends?
4. Do you find it difficult to relax and do nothing on vacations? Do you get depressed when you're still for a period of time?
5. Do you have trouble sleeping because your mind is preoccupied with your work?

POWER/CONTROL

1. Do you have strong opinions about many things, to the point that you find it difficult to see the value in other people's opinions?
2. Would others say you have difficulty reaching compromises?
3. Are you a perfectionist? Do other people find you hard to please?

Personal Assessment: Dependency on Men's Approval

1. Do you find it easier to talk to men than to women?
   Yes _____   No _____
2. At social gatherings, do you interact differently with men than women? If yes, in what way?
   Yes _____   No _____
3. Do you act differently when men are around than when only women are? If yes, in what way?
   Yes _____   No _____
4. At social gatherings or in public, do you notice the men more than the women?
   Yes _____   No _____

5. Do you think about how men will perceive you when you dress or groom?
   Yes ___   No ___
6. Do you react strongly (e.g., rage or depression) when men are critical of you or are angry with you?
   Yes ___   No ___
7. Do you make deliberate eye contact with men in public (e.g., in a store, on the street)?
   Yes ___   No ___
8. If you answered yes to question 7, do you look for some positive signal or response from men through their eye contact with you?
   Yes ___   No ___
9. Has your husband, or have others, ever told you that you're flirtatious?
   Yes ___   No ___

Chapter 7

1. Chapter 7 discusses the need to make amends for those wrong attitudes and things we have done. How do you feel when you consider the possibility of making amends to your husband, in light of the hurt you feel?
2. We make amends to accept personal responsibility for our past behavior, as well as to clear our relationship with God. Have your actions or attitudes hurt your husband or someone else? Are there things that you haven't taken responsibility for? What are those things? List as many as you can think of and ask God to bring to mind any you may have missed or forgotten.
3. How do you feel about making amends for your list? Are you ready to take that step? If not, ask God to help you become ready, and he will lead you in this possibility.

4. Can you forgive yourself for your wrongs? If not, what can you do to begin giving yourself the same grace God gives you?

Chapter 8

1. Do you recognize any of the emotions that are associated with the grief cycle in your own feelings and actions? Which emotions are you experiencing now?
2. Do you feel anger at God? If so, how does that make you feel about yourself?
3. Have you tried to hold your emotions in because you don't know what to do with them?
4. How do you feel about Mark Laaser's belief that the spouse *must* look into her past and grieve old losses, in order for her and her husband to heal as a couple?
5. Do you have a support group to be there for you as you grieve your pain stemming from your husband's behavior and also from old losses?
6. Are you willing to work through the grieving process, knowing that in the end it leads to healing?

The exercises below are tools that help us examine the pain we carry with us. Sometimes we are unaware that it's even there, yet it affects us emotionally and can interfere with our relationships. As you work through them, ask God to give you insight.

Childhood Messages

All of us experience some degree of hurt growing up because we are raised by imperfect people who did the best job they could as parents. For some, the hurts may have been being labeled with comments like, "You are so stupid!" For others, the hurt may be deeper and more damaging, such as being abused sexually. But all these hurts, great or small, affect our view of ourselves; if they are not dealt with, they can inhibit our ability to be "real" around people and take the risks necessary to try new things and grow. Take a few minutes and think about labels and/or hurts you experienced growing up.

Labels I Was Given or Hurts I Experienced

1. _____

   _____

2. _____
3. _____
4. _____
5. _____

Write in detail at least one incident involving a deep hurt you experienced in your childhood. In which of the ways listed below did you respond to that hurt? When old hurts are brought to mind, take a few minutes to think through your reactions to them.

Acted like I was not hurt	Felt rejected/embarrassed
Withdrew	Felt responsible
Cried	Got angry
Told someone	Other

The Gift of Grieving by Jack McGinnis

God gave us the grieving process as a tool to heal our hurts. Making an effort to grieve losses changes their hold on us and enables us to act *and* re-act in more healthy, adult ways. It also lightens the emotional load we carry through our lives. The questions below may help you begin the grieving process.

1. Think about the event in childhood that you wrote about during the above self-test. What were your feelings when it happened?

2. Clearly identify what you lost because of that event. Innocence? Trust?
3. What are your feelings now about your loss from that event?
4. If your original response to the event was to pretend it didn't happen, what have been the consequences of dealing with it that way?
5. Who do you consider, *in your perception*, to be responsible for your loss? Yourself? Another person? God?
6. Where are you in the process of forgiving whoever you consider responsible?
7. Is there a risk in forgiving that person? If so, what is the risk to you?
8. Are you willing, with the help of God and your friends, to take the risk of forgiving that person? (Take the time you need to become willing to forgive. Premature forgiveness short-circuits the grieving process.)

How Do We Go about Healthy Grieving?

1. *By sharing the pain of our lives with other people.* When you share your pain with me, I begin to care about you in a deeper way. This care carries with it healing power, healing love. Some believe that sharing our stories of loss is "wallowing in our past." I disagree. I believe that every time we share our story in a loving environment, we experience healing.
2. *By feeling and expressing our feelings.* I believe God has given each of us a grieving system to help us deal with losses in life, just as he's given us an immune system to help us deal with dangerous infections. Feelings give energy to that grieving system. When we freely feel, we energize our grieving system to do its work.
3. *By openly grieving with the help of a trusted friend.* When we allow ourselves to openly grieve, identify losses, express our feelings, and come to forgiveness

207

or closure, we utilize the grieving system in a way that gives it energy and helps it work better.

4. *By praying for healing for our grieving system.* Some of our grieving systems were overloaded and damaged when we were children. God wants to heal us. If we don't grieve well, we can ask God to heal our grieving system so the process will gift us.

5. *By grieving one loss at a time.* I discovered my grieving system could not work at one time because of all the losses I had sustained. I have discovered that by taking my losses one at a time, I don't have to go to every event. The miracle of grace and healing makes it possible for the completion of one event to affect many like it. The image that comes to my mind is of dropping a pebble into water. Concentric circles radiate from the center. Likewise, grieving the losses I sustained in one or two major events touches many others like it in my life and heals them as well.

One of the most important dimensions of grieving is forgiveness. In order to complete the grieving of a loss, I have to come to the point of forgiving the person I hold responsible for the loss. Often, we are tempted to jump ahead to forgiveness before we have done our feeling work. The willingness to forgive is important, but if forgiveness is premature, it is not complete. I believe forgiveness comes at the end of the process, as a gift. The grieving system actually *delivers* forgiveness. What changes for me, then, is the way I carry the event or the person. Likewise, it is important to process only one loss at a time, because it is possible to forgive the same person for one event or loss, but not to have forgiven them for other events or losses.

If you have been stuck in the agony of hurt and pain from the losses you've sustained, I pray that you will soon be able to complete the work of healthy grieving, to let go of those frozen feelings and to make space for grace.

May your grieving give you life![1]

Chapter 9

As you answer these questions, apply them to your relationship with your husband. If you wish to apply them to other relationships, do so at a later time.

1. What does the word *forgiveness* mean to you?
2. Why do you think forgiveness needs to be our goal in all our relationships?
3. Do you agree with Lewis Smedes's statement that when you forgive, "You set a prisoner free, but you discover that the real prisoner was yourself"?
4. Do you think that you tend to forgive too quickly, refuse to consider forgiving, are passive about the work involved, or just need more time for the forgiveness process? Why?
5. What is your response to Eileen's statement in chapter 9 that "the ground is level at the foot of the cross. Without the cross, we're all lost. Not just those with sexual addictions—all of us"?
6. Do you think you'll ever be able to trust your husband again? Why or why not?
7. Several women in chapter 9 allow their husbands to be honest with them when they feel tempted or give into temptation, and can do so without being judgmental. Do you think an accountability relationship with your husband is healthy in your marriage, or do you think it would be better for your husband to find another honest man to be accountable with?
8. Can you live with the fact that there are no guarantees that your husband won't fail again? Why or why not?

9. Can you ask God to meet you wherever you are in relation to forgiving your husband? Can you accept his grace for you in that position, knowing he's at work in your life?

10. Are you willing to leave your heart and mind open to God's healing, knowing that he can move you toward forgiveness?

Chapter 10

1. Can you identify with the quote from *Alice's Adventures in Wonderland* at the opening of this chapter? Do you, too, feel somewhat "lost"? Describe those feelings.

2. Do you believe your marriage is going to survive? Why or why not?

3. If your marriage ends in divorce, do you know where to find emotional and spiritual support?

4. Do you recognize the in-between time of transition in your own life right now? Explain what that is like for you.

5. In what ways do you feel vulnerable right now?

6. What mementos or keepsakes do you have that bring reminders that you are loved and valuable? What are your positive qualities that these keepsakes reflect?

7. When you journal, what thoughts and feelings seem to reappear most often? What does that tell you about your needs right now?

8. Do you currently have an outlet for helping others in some way? If so, what do you gain from this activity?

9. What new choices and opportunities would you like to explore? Can you feel yourself "thawing" emotionally as Juanita's poem "The Wind" describes?

Chapter 11

1. How might you be "Jesus with skin on" to another woman who is experiencing the raw pain you felt when you began this growing process? Do you think that you have something to offer such a woman, and that you would probably receive something back in the exchange? Why or why not?
2. What do you feel when you read Sandy Wilson's comments as quoted at the end of chapter 11 and reproduced below?

As I drink in the beauty of this crisp fall day, I am awed that I feel so at peace and so thankful for my life. Seven years ago, when my world shattered through the revelations of my husband's unfaithfulness, no one could have convinced me that I would ever celebrate life again.

Appendix 3

Resource Directory

Dr. Mark Laaser, whose book *Faithful and True* is quoted repeatedly in this book, conducts intensive seminars throughout the country on sexual addiction recovery. He can be reached at:

The Christian Alliance for Sexual Recovery
P.O. Box 2124
Tupelo, MS 38803-2124
(601) 844-5128

American Family Association is a Christian organization with a branch that helps couples dealing with sexual betrayal and sex addiction. They offer a variety of materials and training for both men and women struggling with sexual issues, as well as for their spouses. The AFA can be reached at:

American Family Association
P.O. Drawer 2440
Tupelo, MS 38803
(800) 326-4543
Web site: afa.net

Elizabeth Harris, whose story we told, cowrote a workbook called *A Journey to Peace: Help for Women in Relationship with a Sexually Addicted Man*. This workbook is a valuable tool for any woman whose husband struggles with sexual issues. It costs twenty-five dollars and can be ordered through the AFA.

Juanita Ryan, whose poems appear in this book, is a counselor, poet, and writer in the Los Angeles area. She can be reached by calling her counseling office at: (714) 257-1357.

Juanita's husband, Dale Ryan, is the CEO of Christian Recovery International, which is the parent organization for The National Association for Christian Recovery (NACR). Among other resources, the NACR publishes *STEPS: The Magazine of Hope and Healing for Christians in Recovery. STEPS* is a quarterly publication and is a valuable tool in the healing and growth process. This organization also sponsors conferences and edits a resource directory, among other things. They may be reached at:

The National Association for Christian Recovery
P.O. Box 215
Brea, CA 92822-0215
(714) 529-6227
E-mail: hopehappens@earthlink.net
Web site: http://www.christianrecovery.com

Earl and Sandy Wilson, whose story appears in several places in this book, live and work in the Portland, Oregon area. Earl is a psychologist and part-time professor at Trinity Western University, and Sandy is a counselor, conference speaker, and instructor of counseling at Western Seminary. They are the coauthors of *Restoring the Fallen* and train spiritual care teams for helping couples who've gone through the devastation of sexual betrayal. They help connect hurting couples with teams to lead them through the healing process. Earl and Sandy can be reached at:

Wilson Counseling Service
(503) 659-4082

Richard and Pam Crist, whose story appears throughout this book, are a husband and wife counseling team. They do marriage and family counseling, work with groups of husbands and groups of wives, and speak to other groups, as well. They can be reached by contacting:

Crist Family Ministries
23324 32nd Ave. W.
Brier, WA 98036
(360) 794-2529

Marnie Ferree, whose story appears in chapter 6, is a marriage and family counselor, conducts intensive seminars for female sex addicts, and is currently writing a book about her recovery journey. Marnie can be reached at the address below:

Marnie Ferree, M.A.
Woodmont Hills Counseling Ministry
3422 Golf Club Lane
Nashville, TN 37215
(615) 269-6220

Carol Anderson and Jim Shores minister through Acts of Renewal, a husband and wife drama team that has performed for *Focus on the Family* and many other national Christian ministries. Carol and Jim allowed me to share their remarkable recovery story in the pages of this book. They can be reached for information about their ministry at: (864) 421-9500.

Sharon Hersh's story is told in chapter 6. She is a counselor in Denver, Colorado. You can reach Sharon at:

Cherry Creek Counseling Center
3665 Cherry Creek Dr. N., Suite 290
Denver, CO 80209
(303) 799-6815

Dr. Doug Weiss is executive director of Heart to Heart Counseling Center in Ft. Worth, Texas. He offers counseling, books, and videos on sexual addiction recovery for men and women. For more information, call (817) 377-4278, or visit his web site (http://www.sexaddict.com).

My husband, Pat Means, author of *Men's Secret Wars,* and my cohost on our radio show *Love Under Fire,* presents Men's Secret Wars seminars nationally on the subject of sexual integrity. Pat also conducts church training seminars on how to establish and lead sexual addiction recovery support groups. I present a women's seminar for general audiences entitled Women, Romance and Integrity, as well as an intensive workshop for wives of sex addicts. Together, Pat and I present seminars on the principles of healthy marriage. You can reach us at:

Courageous Living
P.O. Box 2259
Redmond, WA 98073
(800) 252-6055

Some other useful addresses follow.

Twelve Step Groups

Participating in a Twelve Step recovery program is crucial for achieving and maintaining sobriety. There are several fellowships for sexual addiction:

For addicts:
Sexaholics Anonymous (SA)
P.O. Box 11910
Nashville, TN 37222-1910
(615) 331-6230
www.sa.org

Sex Addicts Anonymous (SAA)
P.O. Box 70949
Houston, TX 77270
(713) 869-4902
www.sexaa.org

Sex and Love Addicts Anonymous (SLAA)
P.O. Box 650010
West Newton, MA 02165-0010
(617) 332-1845

Overcomers Outreach (Christian group for any addiction)
520 N. Brockhurst STE 121
Anaheim, CA 92801
(714) 491-3000

For co-addicts:
S-Anon International Family Groups (S-Anon)
P.O. Box 111242
Nashville, TN 37222-1242
(615) 833-3152

Codependents of Sex Addicts (COSA)
9337 B Katy Fwy #142
Houston, TX 77204
(612) 537-6904

For couples:
Recovering Couples Anonymous (RCA)
P.O. Box 11872
St. Louis, MO 63105
(314) 830-2600

For sexual trauma survivors:
Survivors of Incest Anonymous (SIA)
P.O. Box 21817
Baltimore, MD 21222
(410) 282-3400

Incest Survivors Anonymous (ISA)
P.O. Box 17245
Long Beach, CA 90807
(562) 428-5599

For information and referrals on sexual addiction:
National Council on Sexual Addiction and Compulsivity (NCSAC)
P.O. Box 161064
Atlanta, GA 30321-9998
(770) 968-5002
www.ncsac.org

Notes

Chapter 1

1. H. B. London Jr. and Neil B. Wiseman, *Pastors at Risk* (Wheaton: Victor, 1993), 22.

2. "Christianity Today Marriage and Divorce Survey Report," Christianity Today, Inc., Research Dept., July 1992, 15.

3. Mark Laaser, *The Secret Sin* (Grand Rapids: Zondervan, 1992), 21.

4. Patrick Carnes, *Out of the Shadows* (Minneapolis: Comp Care Publications, 1993), 4.

5. Ibid.

6. Patrick Means, *Men's Secret Wars* (Grand Rapids: Revell, 1996), 126.

7. *Sexaholics Anonymous* (Simi Valley, Calif.: Sexaholics Literature, 1988), 45.

8. Robin Norwood, *Women Who Love Too Much* (New York: Pocket Books, 1986), 214–15.

9. Mark Luciano and Christopher Merris, *If Only You Would Change* (Nashville: Thomas Nelson, 1992), 13.

10. Melody Beattie, *Codependent No More* (San Francisco: Harper/Hazelden, 1987), 103.

11. Jennifer Schneider, *Back from Betrayal* (New York: Ballantine Books, 1988), 193.

12. Luciano and Merris, *If Only You Would Change,* 85–86.

13. Norwood, *Women Who Love Too Much,* 254.

Chapter 2

1. Millwem, *Women's Groups: How Connections Heal* (Stone Center, Wellesley College, 1986), 5.

2. Ibid.

3. Schneider, *Back from Betrayal,* 189.

4. Curt Grayson and Jan Johnson, *Creating Safe Places* (San Francisco: HarperSanFrancisco, 1991), 163.

Chapter 3

1. Luciano and Merris, *If Only You Would Change,* 9.
2. Ibid., 15.
3. Nancy Groom, *From Bondage to Bonding* (Colorado Springs: NavPress, 1991), 100.
4. Ibid., 20.
5. Ibid., 90.
6. Ibid., 48.
7. Walter Hooper, ed., *C. S. Lewis Readings for Meditation and Reflection* (San Francisco: HarperSanFrancisco, 1992), 192.
8. Groom, *From Bondage to Bonding,* 200.

Chapter 4

1. Dr. Harry Schaumburg, *False Intimacy* (Colorado Springs: NavPress, 1994), 113.
2. Ibid.
3. Mark Laaser, *Faithful and True* (Grand Rapids: Zondervan, 1992), 138.
4. David Augsburger, "The F Word," *STEPS: The Magazine of Hope and Healing for Christians in Recovery* 8, no. 3 (fall 1997): 7.
5. James Dobson, *Love Must Be Tough* (Nashville: Word, 1996), 54–55.
6. Groom, *From Bondage to Bonding,* 110.
7. Dobson, *Love Must Be Tough,* 59–60.
8. Ibid., 49.
9. Schaumburg, *False Intimacy,* 116.
10. Willard Harley, *His Needs, Her Needs* (Grand Rapids: Revell, 1986), 162.
11. Dobson, *Love Must Be Tough,* 30, 60.
12. Ibid., 60.
13. Schaumburg, *False Intimacy,* 113.
14. Laaser, *Faithful and True,* 141.
15. Dobson, *Love Must Be Tough,* 63.
16. Ibid., 62.

Chapter 5

1. Gloria G. Harris and Rona Subotnik, *Surviving Infidelity: Making Decisions, Recovering from the Pain* (Holbrook, Mass.: Adams Publishing, 1973), 67.

2. Alan Loy McGinnis, *Confidence* (Minneapolis: Augsburg, 1987), 25.

3. Ibid., 125.

4. Colette Dowling, *Perfect Women* (New York: Summit Books, 1988), 213.

5. Richard Dickinson and Carol Gift Page, *The Child in Each of Us* (Wheaton: Victor, 1977), 18.

6. Source unknown.

7. Earl and Sandy Wilson, Paul and Virginia Friesen, Larry and Nancy Paulson, *Restoring the Fallen* (Downers Grove, Ill.: InterVarsity Press, 1992), 95–96.

8. Harris and Subotnik, *Surviving Infidelity*, 165.

9. McGinnis, *Confidence*, 82, 84–85.

10. Ron Lee Davis, *Courage to Begin Again* (Eugene, Oreg.: Harvest House, 1988), 123.

Chapter 6

1. Michael Moore, M.S., from foreword to Cynthia Rowland McClure, *The Courage to Go On* (Grand Rapids: Baker, 1990), 9.

2. McClure, *The Courage to Go On*, 29.

3. Luciano and Merris, *If Only You Would Change*, 65.

4. Groom, *From Bondage to Bonding*, 90.

5. McClure, *The Courage to Go On*, 37.

6. Lynda Kline, *Focus on the Family with Dr. James Dobson*, July 1998.

7. McClure, *The Courage to Go On*, 46.

Chapter 7

1. Schneider, *Back from Betrayal*, 198.

2. David Augsburger, "The F Word," *STEPS: The Magazine of Hope and Healing for Christians in Recovery* 8, no. 3 (fall 1997): 4.

3. Luciano and Merris, *If Only You Would Change*, 179–80.

Chapter 8

1. Dean Ornish, M.D., *Prevention Magazine*, August 1998, 116, 200.

2. Dobson, *Love Must Be Tough*, 21.

3. Dave Carder and Duncan Jaeniche, *Torn Asunder: Recovering from Extramarital Affairs* (Chicago: Moody, 1992), 173.

4. Ibid.

5. Ibid., 174.

6. Schaumburg, *False Intimacy,* 107.

7. Harriet Lerner, *The Dance of Anger* (New York: Harper & Row, 1985), 5.

8. Laaser, *Faithful and True,* chapter 12.

9. Dowling, *Perfect Women,* 213.

Chapter 9

1. Lewis Smedes, *Forgive and Forget* (New York: Pocket Books, 1990), 114.

2. Augsburger, *STEPS,* 5.

3. Smedes, *Forgive and Forget,* xii.

4. Ibid., 133.

5. Ibid., 108.

6. Augsburger, *STEPS,* 6.

7. Smedes, *Forgive and Forget,* 39.

8. Ibid., 131.

9. Augsburger, *STEPS,* 4.

10. Jack McGinnis, *STEPS* 3, no. 1 (spring 1992): 11.

11. Juanita Ryan, *STEPS: The Magazine of Hope and Healing for Christians in Recovery* 8, no. 3 (fall 1997): 11.

12. Smedes, *Forgive and Forget,* 23.

13. McGinnis, *Confidence,* 114.

14. Lewis Smedes, *STEPS: The Magazine of Hope and Healing for Christians in Recovery* 8, no. 3 (fall 1997): 15.

15. Augsburger, *STEPS,* 6.

16. Smedes, *Forgive and Forget,* 34.

Chapter 10

1. William Bridges, *Transitions: Making Sense of Life's Changes* (New York: Addison-Wesley, 1980), 13.

2. Ibid., 11.

3. Ibid., 4.

Chapter 11

1. David Parington, *Making the Break* (Wheaton: Harold Shaw Publishers, 1984), 51–52.

2. "A Hunger for Healing" Video Series (Colorado Springs: NavPress/Piñon Press).

3. Wilson, Friesen, and Paulson, *Restoring the Fallen,* 93.

Appendix 1

1. Adapted from *Celebrate Recovery Leader's Guide and Training Manual* by John Baker (Mission Viejo, Calif.: Celebrate Recovery Books, 1996), 25.

Appendix 2

1. Jack McGinnis, "The Gift of Grieving," *STEPS* (spring 1992): 14–15.

Marsha Means, M.A., is a marriage and family therapist and a frequent speaker to women's groups. Marsha is cofounder, with her husband, Pat, of Prodigals International, a Seattle-based ministry to individuals and couples impacted by sexual addiction. For more information on Prodigals International, visit their web site at www.iProdigals.com.

Men's Secret Wars

Patrick A. Means

Many men are fighting secret wars— against workaholism, sexual addiction, substance abuse, pornography, and extramarital affairs. They are often reluctant to seek help, and find their battles difficult to win because of baggage from the past and pressures in the present. But men don't have to become casualties in these secret wars.

This book helps readers recognize the "at risk" factors that precede the development of a secret life. Drawing candidly from his own struggles and those of numerous other men, Patrick Means provides tested strategies for defeating the habits and secrets that threaten men's private lives. A leader's guide has been added to this paperback edition.

Pat Means is president of Prodigals International, cofounder of the National Association for Christian Recovery, the former U.S. director of Campus Crusade for Christ, and a frequent speaker to men's groups. Pat and his wife, Marsha, live and work in Seattle, Washington. For more information on Prodigals International, visit their web site at www.iProdigals.com.

0-8007-5717-3   288 pages $12.99p